THE ARTS
DO WE NEED THEM?

THE ARTS

DO WE NEED THEM?

Louis A. Gill

Franklin Watts
London/New York/Sydney/Toronto

© Franklin Watts Ltd 1990
First published by Franklin Watts Ltd
96 Leonard Street
London EC2A 4RH
ISBN: 0 7496 0285 6
Design: Edward Kinsey
Editor: Jenny Wood
Typeset by J&L Composition Ltd, Filey, North Yorkshire
Printed by Guernsey Press, Channel Islands

CONTENTS

Introduction 7

1
The context – setting the scene 11

2
The case for the arts 25

3
The creative process and the role of the teacher 42

4
The expressive arts and the National Curriculum 59

Appendix: a timetable model 84

5
Assessment and evaluation 91

6
Providing the teachers 109

7
Artists in education 127

8
Towards a policy for the arts 144

9
Effecting change 165

Bibliography 179

Index 181

To
Margaret

INTRODUCTION

'The arts – do we need them?' At the risk of disappointing the reader who enjoys surprise and who thrives on the self-discipline which overcomes the temptation to turn to the last page for a solution, the short answer to the question is 'Yes!'. The purpose of this book is, of course, to elaborate on this initial, succinct response, and to do so four aims have been used to provide a framework:

a) *To clarify thinking on key issues related to arts education and arts provision*

The first need is to identify clearly that in this context 'the arts' refers to the expressive disciplines, i.e. dance, drama, music, the verbal arts and the visual arts (including film and photography). The second need is for a shared understanding of the term 'arts education'. A distinction is made here between the *educational* function of the arts and the *social* function. It is the former which is central to any truly balanced curriculum. Arts education is concerned with awareness (in all its forms), with the acknowledgement and identification of a feeling response to a stimulus, and with the structured expression of that response. Through arts education, and the development of the arts experience, other awarenesses are given a sharper focus leading the pupil to a deeper understanding of the environment, of other people, other cultures and the works of other artists. The affective approach can inform and broaden the range of enquiry in other curriculum areas. The uniqueness of the arts experience provides 'another way of knowing'.

This interpretation of 'arts education' may be at variance with the experiences of some heads, teachers, parents and governors who perceive the arts in terms of the diet they received as pupils. Hence there is a need to establish a shared understanding of the terms used.

Throughout the book the arts experience is given pride of place over any individual discipline. The separate disciplines are seen as paths leading to that experience, and in that sense they are both subservient to and essential to the arts experience. The health and well-being of the discrete art forms is crucial, just as the condition of the organs in the body is vital to the health of the individual.

The challenge within the expressive arts curriculum is to establish a balance between breadth of study, which enables the pupil to interrelate disciplines and appreciate the distinct qualities of each, and depth of study, which equips the pupil with the skills to think and communicate fluently in a particular medium.

b) *To provoke sufficient theoretical and philosophical discussion to underpin policy and curriculum decisions*

A key word in this aim is 'sufficient'. It is not the purpose here to immerse the reader in deep philosophical discussion. At the same time there is a need to encourage a deeper exploration and understanding of the nature of the arts, of arts education and of the processes and relationships involved, for only then can the question 'Why?' be satisfactorily answered and sound curriculum decisions reached. The alternative is the perpetuation of curricula built on hunches and past habits.

To assist and inform discussion, there is a chapter outlining a case for the arts in education and a further chapter describing the nature of the creative process. Other sections relate to providing opportunities for experience as well as for the acquisition of skills, and the value of artist residencies is discussed. There is also a chapter on appropriate forms of assessment, recording and reporting. The focal theme of such debate and consultation should be the need to produce a statement of entitlement relating to *all* pupils in a school, regardless of age or ability level, and from the statement should emerge a set of aims which influence all dimensions of school life (i.e. including the hidden curriculum, the ambience of the school, etc.).

c) *To suggest routes capable of leading to practical results – to provide actions and intentions with a purpose and direction*

In many team games the formation of the team is arranged to fulfil three functions: there are defenders, mid-field players, and attackers. The role of the mid-field player is to build from defence into attack – to create opportunities for attack. The world of education has its parallel, with the educational philosophers providing the defence and the classroom teachers the attack. Between the two are the enablers – those who give philosophy curriculum shape; who make things happen; who devise strategies for overcoming problems and circumventing opposition.

It is a major purpose of this book to attempt the mid-field role – to identify and advocate processes and approaches which can be practically and effectively applied; to suggest routes which provide access to a coherent expressive arts curriculum.

To map these routes, consideration is given to an arts policy (at school, LEA, and national level), to the construction of the curriculum, to timetabling and to the questions of organisation and co-ordination. Some thought is also given to the relationship between the school and the community. Of course, there is no single route suitable for all schools, if only for the reason that each and every school has a different point of departure. But there is enough information here – there are enough pointers – to lead even the inexperienced traveller, and yet sufficient diversions to challenge the intrepid.

d) *To advocate a strong contempt for the impossible and a determination to take full advantage of the opportunities presented within a changing scene*

This book was originally prompted by a positive feeling of optimism for the expressive arts – a clear conviction that the arts have a future. A number of factors contributed to that belief. First, there has been a pronounced change of mood during the past four or five years. Until then arts teachers had been almost constantly on the defensive and were often regarded as lightweights in the staffroom – sometimes with subversive intent! Increasingly the arts are being acknowledged as equal partners with other areas of experience within a balanced curriculum, and dissident arts teachers are being invited in from the cold. Slowly but surely the unique contribution of the arts is being appreciated, and with that recognition the confidence of arts teachers is growing. (There is a strange irony in the fact that it is the tightening grip of technology and vocational training which has ultimately led to the reappraisal of the value of the expressive disciplines.)

Second, some recognition of the arts' status has been confirmed within the list of National Curriculum foundation subjects. Of course the hierarchical division of the arts within that list is deplorable – and we obviously return to that theme later – but few of us expected both art and music to find favour at the time when the National Curriculum plans were first being formulated.

Third, there is a growing spirit of camaraderie among arts teachers, and both within staffrooms and through organised conferences and seminars dialogue and discussion are encouraging greater mutual understanding which must inevitably lead to increased curricular coherence.

Most importantly, the traditional curriculum mould has been broken by the introduction of the National Curriculum, and it is transparently clear that historical curriculum models will not solve present needs. New approaches are essential – through overlapping subject areas, examining cross-curricular possibilities, exploring modular constructions, timeblocks, etc. – to make sense of a curriculum which is outwardly extremely divisive but inwardly offers the potential for a degree of unity which has not previously characterised English education (at least, not at secondary level). In this climate of curriculum instability the time is opportune for the expressive arts teacher to influence significantly the shape of things to come.

Of course, some teachers see the overcrowding of the timetable as a threat to the arts, and it must be true – particularly if the *National Curriculum* is confused with the *whole* curriculum – that if schools persist with an outmoded approach, the sum of the parts will be much greater than the available whole and something will have to give. Let us not be deluded, the expressive arts never have had a glorious heyday, although individual disciplines in individual schools would no doubt argue otherwise. We are considering here the expressive arts as a generic group, and providing the case is thoroughly prepared and competently argued the full flowering has yet to come. The opportunities for change must not be missed.

The final chapter offers thoughts and advice on the process of effecting change.

CHAPTER 1 THE CONTEXT – SETTING THE SCENE

There have probably been more changes in education during the past four years than in the preceding forty – a combined total which conveniently bridges the period between the 1944 Education Act and the Education Reform Act of 1988. Few of the recent changes have been cosmetic. Several – such as the introduction of the General Certificate of Secondary Education, the extension of the Technical and Vocational Education Initiative, the introduction of the Grant Related In-Service Training scheme (now the Local Education Authority Training Grant Scheme) and various Educational Support Grant strategies – have penetrated to the very roots of the system and consequently have disturbed the growth patterns established over a long period. And, of course, there are more – many more – to come as the impact of the 1988 Act unfolds.

In the face of yet more change, the mood within the teaching profession is mixed and not easy to assess. The layperson can afford extravagant opinions, informed or otherwise. But the practitioner is charged with delivering the product and will tend to temper excessive enthusiasm with caution, mindful of the complexities of the educational process, particularly at a time when all of the constituent elements of that process appear in themselves to be vulnerable to change. For the teacher, the concern is not only with *what* the National Curriculum will comprise, but also *how* it will be managed.

For the expressive arts teacher there is the additional uncertainty caused by being at the end of the National Curriculum agenda (i.e. the date for implementation is autumn 1992). There is an understandable fear that important curriculum decisions will have been made at an early stage, and that the arts could be left with restricted opportunities.

To understand the present situation it is helpful to reflect on some of the more significant changes in education which have occurred since 1944, particularly in so far as they have affected the arts.

The grammar school and the arts

The first ten to fifteen years of this period were very much concerned with establishing the tri-partite system introduced by the 1944 Act (i.e. the division of secondary education into grammar schools, secondary modern schools, and technical high schools). A major consequential impact on the junior school curriculum was the inevitable focusing on the 11+ examination – the process by which pupils at the age of 11 could be categorised 'by age, aptitude and ability' and allocated to one or other of the three types of secondary school. Despite the good intentions of the Act, inability to secure a place in the grammar school was seen as social failure and the parental pressure on children to 'succeed' was in some instances quite unreasonable. The sense of achievement experienced by a pupil on 'getting into the grammar school' often encouraged an exaggerated loyalty to, and pride in, the school. Tradition was all important and something to be valued far beyond school-leaving day – hence the proliferation of old grammarians' associations. Within the grammar schools, the majority of which were single sex schools, pupils on entry were again streamed according to ability, the lowest stream frequently being viewed with a degree of disdain both by superior peers and by academically motivated teachers. In most grammar schools scholarship and sporting prowess provided the educational goals – the latter being of particular significance in the boys' grammar school. Not surprisingly, there was invariably a strong competitive spirit.

In such a climate there was little encouragement for the expressive arts within the taught curriculum. Art and music were usually included during the first two, sometimes three, years but drama and dance had no place except in a very few enlightened schools. The value attached to arts subjects was reflected by the readiness with which they were sacrificed to accommodate, for example, extra science or extra language teaching. Nor were they recognised by most universities for matriculation purposes.

But status was not the sole problem. The style of arts teaching also left much to be desired. Music, in particular, was often taught badly. The class singing lesson, inherited from the pre-war years, was slow to die and not infrequently music lessons degenerated into an opportunity for hymn practice for morning assemblies. The *National Song Book* still retained pride of place in the music room. In adventurous schools this diet was sometimes supplemented with the occasional theory lesson and, perhaps, a little music history or music appreciation. Creative music-making in the classroom was, for the most part, unheard of in the grammar school.

Whilst art lessons generally offered much greater scope for expressive work they often seemed to be designed for the specialist draughtsperson, leaving many pupils feeling inadequate and frustrated. It is not surprising that so few continued with expressive arts subjects beyond the age of 14.

Outside the classroom artistic standards were often high. This was the period which witnessed the introduction and growth of peripatetic instrumental teaching. Prize Days and Speech Days provided show-case opportunities for the arts, and the school calendar would usually include choral and orchestral concerts as well as drama (and sometimes 'operatic') productions. The message was clear: the arts were good for the public image of the school, but should not be allowed to detract from the more serious business of learning.

It is worth pausing for a moment to absorb the important fact that, until very recently, the vast majority of headteachers would themselves have been products of the grammar school system – and so too would teachers, governors, parents and politicians. Many benefited greatly from their grammar school education. It provided a passport to a university place, to a good job or to a profession. Personal success, combined with the sense of loyalty and tradition inculcated by the system, created a barrier to change which was only slowly penetrated – very slowly in the case of the expressive arts. Experience is a much stronger persuader than rational argument, and the negative arts experiences imbibed during the grammar school years often insidiously fostered attitudes which have been – and still are – difficult to overcome. The Gulbenkian Report comments: *'Many administrators, headteachers, parents, teachers and pupils, have failed to see the value of the arts – in many cases, we believe, because of their own indifferent experiences of them at school'.*

(It is an incidental but important additional point to make that the term 'arts education' can have a variety of interpretations, coloured by personal experience. Those from a background where the arts education had a somewhat narrow focus may well have a less generous understanding of the term than the younger reader. Certainly it has been my experience in discussions with heads and others that, although we have been using a common vocabulary, the impacted meanings of the words we have been using sometimes differed widely. It is necessary to establish a clear definition, and a shared definition, if meaningful discussion is to take place. Such a definition will emerge from later chapters.)

Child-centred developments
Whilst the grammar schools were educating future headteachers and teachers by recycling traditional academic curricula, schools less directly governed by the demands of external examination syllabuses and less dominated by university requirements had a somewhat freer hand. For a variety of reasons secondary modern schools were a far less homogeneous group than the grammar schools. The best were enlightened establishments in which exciting educational developments took place. They rejected the image of 'second-class grammar school' and created imaginative and independent identities with curricula appropriate to the needs of their pupils. The worst were educational sinks and were thorns in the flesh of their LEAs.

It was in the better secondary modern schools, and in the more adventurous junior schools which refused to be hamstrung by the 11+ examination, that educational change was being brought about. Slowly but surely as the 1950s merged into the 1960s the emphasis moved away from 'the system' towards the needs of the child. Education became essentially child-centred, and freedom of expression replaced the rigorous discipline of the previous decade. Unfortunately, the new mood was all too often abused, and 'freedom' on occasions gave way to 'chaos'. The expressive arts were as prone, if not more prone, to these excesses as any other area of the curriculum. The visual arts and creative writing were particularly vulnerable.

The innovations and experimental activities of the period were synthesised and encapsulated in four events which were to make a significant and lasting impact on the history of education in this country. These were:

- the change to a comprehensive school system;
- the raising of the school-leaving age;

- the introduction of the Certificate of Secondary Education;
- the birth of a new expression, 'curriculum development'.

The emergence of the term 'curriculum development' seemed somehow to generate a new impetus towards analysing educational process and curriculum diet. Furthermore, this enthusiasm was nurtured in a period of affluence seldom experienced in education. The early 1970s witnessed an expansion of facilities and equipment unequalled in modern times. For the arts this often meant the provision of open-plan art and craft blocks, purpose-built music areas complete with practice rooms, drama studios and, sometimes, small theatres.

Accountability and functional utilitarianism

The pendulum of change is seldom still in education and by the mid-1970s the age of accountability had dawned. The now famous Callaghan speech at Ruskin College (1976) was perhaps a symptom rather than the cause of changing times. Whatever status we choose to accord to that occasion, it certainly heralded a scrutiny of education hitherto unknown. For some it presented an opportunity to blame education for most of the nation's ills – industrial, economic, social and spiritual. And, of course, critics had little difficulty in finding ammunition among the wilder indulgences of the previous decades. The new era sought to reduce the cost of education and to relate educational practice to the economic needs of the country. Thus in the Green Paper 'Education in Schools: A Consultative Document' (1977) we read: *'Education, like any other public service, is answerable to the society which it serves and which pays for it'*. And further: *'The curriculum in many schools is not sufficiently matched to a life in modern industrial society'*.

The shift of emphasis was clearly signposted. The move was to lead away from the needs of the child *now* and towards the needs of the child *later*, as an adult contributing to the economic growth and viability of the nation. Education therefore needed to be functional, and to justify their share of a shrinking budget all teachers, including the expressive arts teachers, needed to respond positively to this 'instrumental' attitude. This mood had been prevalent for some time prior to 1977, for Ross writing in 1975 (*Arts and the Adolescent*) comments: *'Under pressure to establish themselves within an essentially product-orientated, instrumental, externally validated milieu, arts teachers are seeking a functional utilitarian role'*. He quotes by way of example: *'Art teachers seek to promote visual literacy and regroup as design departments; drama teachers, through role play, 'gaming' and the documentary, feel that they are developing social skills, social consciousness – not to say social conscience'.*

In fact from the mid-1970s, arts teachers have often felt themselves to be in a hostile climate. Economic cuts have, on occasion, threatened job security, and the perceived importance of training rather than education has done little to enhance either individual or collective morale.

The years since 1977 have produced a plethora of papers and reports intended to inform and promote discussions on curriculum development. The list is impressive in length but the characteristic they seem to share is the comparatively scant attention given to the arts. Probably the most significant of these publications for present purposes was the 'Curriculum 11–16' (the 'Red Book'), a working paper produced by a group of HMIs. The writers saw the curriculum *'to be concerned with introducing pupils during the period of compulsory schooling to certain essential "areas of experience"'*. Various reports, including Hadow (1923) and Spens (1938) from the pre-war years, had commended the importance of the arts in the curriculum, but no previous 'official' document had so effectively identified the component elements of a balanced curriculum, one of which was the 'aesthetic and creative'. Indeed, the strength of the proposed curriculum was precisely that – its balance. It was a curriculum framework founded on good sense which few could or would deny. Despite the many pressures which have been exerted on curriculum planning since 1977, some of which we are about to discuss, the essence of the HMI model seems to have survived. Its influence can still be discerned (admittedly with some difficulty) in the 1988 National Curriculum.

In the early 1980s the political scene became increasingly preoccupied with rising unemployment. Swingeing cuts in the education budget were designed to streamline the service and to make it more 'efficient'. Comparisons were made with the education systems of other industrial nations, notably with Germany. Not surprisingly the domestic system fared unfavourably – for obviously no such comparison would have been publicised had there not been a political point to make.

Targeted funding

The consequence of these analyses and comparisons was the introduction of a style of educational change hitherto unknown in this country – educational change by seduction. The coffers of the education service may well have been low, but this did not prevent the Government from making huge funds available through the recently formed Manpower Services Commission. These funds could be tapped by those Local Education Authorities and schools who were prepared to offer schemes for pre-vocational courses along guidelines issued by the MSC. The sums of money available were difficult to resist – hence the element of seduction – and there was considerable disgust in education circles that Central Government should seek to influence the curriculum via the Department of Employment rather than through an adequately funded Department of Education and Science. Indeed, there was a period of uncertainty when it was not clear where the balance of power truly lay.

The danger of a system which relies on targeted funding is that it can, and usually does, distort the balance of the curriculum. By focusing the spotlight on a particular curriculum area or issue, the rest of the curriculum is likely to fall into shadow. The more substantial the funding is, the greater the contrast will be and the deeper the shadow. Thus there was a distinct lurch towards a curriculum which prioritised economic and industrial awareness, and which addressed pre-vocational training.

Coincidentally, secondary schools were finding themselves with a new clientele – the pupils who, at the age of 16, could not find employment, and who wished to return to school for one year to secure qualifications which would have currency value in the shrinking employment market. The examination courses of the Royal Society of Arts and the City and Guilds of London Institute, hitherto used mainly in Colleges of Further Education, began to appear regularly in post-16 curricula and quite quickly were adopted for some pupils in the 14–16 age range as well. In a very short period of time the ethos of comprehensive schools had changed – in some instances quite dramatically. The age distribution reflected the new circumstances and the mould of the traditional academic sixth form had been shattered by the inevitable shift in social balance. Many feared that schools would become training rather than educational establishments.

Targeted funding is, of course, a very powerful tool for any government to use. It combines the twin features of specific focus with maximum accountability. The extension of the TVEI to all secondary schools, the identifying of national priorities within the

Local Education Authority Training Grant Scheme and the extensive use of Educational Support Grants for specific subject or training areas indicate the degree to which such funding has become central to the Government's style of curriculum 'direction' (for the level of intervention has now moved beyond that which could be described merely as 'influence'). The ultimate expression of such intervention is expressed in the creation of the City Technology Colleges.

It would be a gross understatement to observe that the expressive arts have not figured prominently in any of these initiatives. Within the prevailing climate of the 1980s it is not difficult to understand why expressive arts teachers have sometimes felt themselves and their disciplines to be undervalued. With change as the most constant feature, these years have been difficult ones and there is nothing to suggest that the pace will slacken. Already the recently arrived GCSE, still in its first flush, is being rudely elbowed aside by the insistent demands of the National Curriculum.

Positive indicators

There is no doubt that the combined impact of the Education Reform Act and the National Curriculum will be profound. Despite the uncertainties referred to earlier and the difficulties posed by the unequal treatment of the arts among the listed foundation subjects, arts teachers would do well to appreciate that there has never been a potentially more opportune time for the comprehensive development of the arts in schools. The signs are encouraging and positive.

a) Change all around is causing many teachers to examine what their purpose is – for all creeds need dusting from time to time. It is demanding a personal analysis of why the arts are so important and what unique characteristics they can contribute to the experience and education of the individual. In many cases this will be a revision exercise, but some teachers may actually be honestly addressing the question for the first time. Perhaps as accomplished practitioners or performers at school they naturally drifted on to college to continue their studies and, with an air of assumed inevitability, drifted back into education where they have continued to peddle almost by habit what they learned themselves.

The challenge of change can produce a state of shock which in turn can be constructive or destructive. But any shock which causes a teacher to explore the very bedrock of his or her convictions for teaching a particular art form can be no bad thing. A positive response to the questions 'Why am I doing this? What is it all about?' will energise the teacher, and the renewed vitality will be communicated to others. A negative or indecisive response will suggest that the teacher would probably be better employed in some other walk of life and, at the very least, is in need of counselling.

b) Common challenges across the arts are reinforcing and accelerating the need for arts teachers to group together. The traditional subject separation which characterised the grammar school approach was exacerbated during the early days of the accountability purge as each discipline sought out its own salvation. Often this meant aligning with subjects carrying a higher credibility tariff – a development of the syndrome noted by Ross in the extract quoted earlier. Such pressures seldom existed in the junior school where good examples of integrated or combined work have long since been readily available as natural expressions of good primary practice. Increasingly in recent years, secondary schools have demonstrated an interest in the combined arts approach for sound educational reasons. Once subject specialists felt reassured that collaboration would not mean a loss of subject identity, the exploration of common aims and shared concepts became feasible, almost invariably to the mutual benefit of all.

For some, the new enthusiasm for collaboration has been prompted by pragmatism rather than by philosophy. The view is first that, with a limited amount of time available, arts teachers must learn to work together and share and, second, that by coming together as a group arts teachers equip themselves with much greater political clout for negotiating both on the curriculum and on the provision of capitation and resources. Whatever initial reasons brought them together, the fact is that arts teachers in schools are now grouping and collaborating to an extent previously unknown.

c) The GCSE syllabuses are offering opportunities for the introduction of new teaching styles. Furthermore, the indications are that candidates enjoy the flexibility and scope available to them. Any system which successfully motivates both teacher and pupil has much to commend it. But the full impact and the true worth of the GCSE can only be assessed when its influence on teaching styles in earlier years becomes apparent. A willingness to explore different approaches is evident. The prognoses are good.

d) The inclusion of an arts component among the foundation subjects for all pupils to the age of 16 has done much to confirm the importance of the arts within a balanced curriculum. (This is the legacy from the 'Curriculum 11-16' 'areas of experience' referred to earlier). It is sad that such a positive move should have been seriously flawed by the 'shades of the grammar school' style of narrow subject labelling. The hierarchical treatment of the arts disciplines betrays a reluctance even now to accept the concept of an arts experience which welcomes all art forms on equal terms. But since the manner in which the curriculum is delivered will be determined by the individual school, there is scope for coherence to be achieved through imaginative planning at the local level.

The requirement to assess is encouraging arts teachers more seriously to seek and develop *appropriate* tools and assessment models for the task. Where a model is developed on an individual school basis, a collaborative group is much more likely to secure a favourable response for its implementation than is an individual teacher working in isolation.

Curriculum and assessment initiatives will stimulate a sharper focusing on continuity, both in terms of progression through a school and between phases.

e) The Local Education Authority Training Grant Scheme has not only increased the volume of INSET, it has also extended the range of modes of delivery. Despite the demands of National Priorities, INSET is no longer dominated by a menu of courses provided centrally. Instead, schools and individual teachers can identify, construct and programme courses to meet their own specific needs. Not infrequently, this involves observing and discussing the work of other teachers, often in other schools. The in-service training needs of expressive arts teachers are discussed later.

f) The publication of the Gulbenkian Report 'The Arts in Schools' (1982) was most timely. No report could ever have been published in seemingly less auspicious times and yet, with its sheer good sense and sound reasoning, it became an exceedingly influential document and remains a reliable source of reference with which to substantiate and support the case for the arts in education. It was appropriate that, three years later, Dr Ken Robinson, the author of the report, should be appointed Director of the School

Curriculum Development Committee's 'Arts in Schools' project. It is also significant that this project was given no purse from which to support participating LEAs. Local Authorities were required to generate their own funding.

Seventy of the 104 LEAs expressed an early interest in the aims of the project and more than half the LEAs in England and Wales have launched arts projects during the past three years, either as part of the SCDC project or independently. In most cases the project phase is nearing completion, and the experience gained and practices developed are being used to inform agendas for action. Some Authorities have moved further and have created a new permanent post within their Advisory Service for an expressive arts coordinator. Interestingly the *Times Educational Supplement* now has an 'Expressive Arts' heading in its 'Situations Vacant' columns.

The Local Management of Schools

The 1988 Act places the responsibility for school management in the hands of the governing body, which will include an appreciably larger parental representation. The delegation of financial control will also be passed directly to schools to the extent that by 1993 each LEA will retain no more than $7\frac{1}{2}$% of the education budget centrally. The Act also provides for individual shools to opt out of an LEA's control entirely. Thus both the financial power of the LEA and its evolved style of influence will be dramatically changed, and it may well be that the next 'temptation' of the arts teacher will emanate from this shift of power.

There is a great deal of good sense in devolving more control to the individual school, but such total transfer as the present Act requires places an immense burden on headteachers who, by training and by calling, are generally not equipped for that responsibility. Most will cope, because they are able people, but in order to cope many will have to direct their energies away from their strengths – i.e. in curriculum and teaching matters – towards the areas in which they have little or limited expertise (and, perhaps, less enthusiasm). Inevitably these areas in which the head feels least confident will demand a disproportionate amount of time and may delay or inhibit exciting curriculum development which could otherwise be taking place. Conversely, governors drawn from business or industry may well have far more extensive financial experience than the head, but only the layperson's knowledge of education. The success or failure of the revised structure will depend upon the willingness and ability of all parties involved to recognise their respective strengths and weaknesses. It is an intriguing recipe which, given the right mix, makes possible exciting, innovative developments efficiently and effectively managed but which, with the wrong ingredients, can provide a forum for interfering busybodies frustrating the smooth running of the school. Of course, the governing bodies of most schools will fall somewhere on a continuum between these two extremes. But the point should not be lost that increasing authority is being handed to the amateur.

The implications for expressive arts teachers are considerable. Would the 'Arts in Schools' initiatives undertaken by so many LEAs have been possible from a central purse reduced to $7\frac{1}{2}$% of the education budget? Can we envisage governing bodies sustaining the level of peripatetic instrumental teaching currently provided by LEAs? If they do, will tuition be free? Will the level of support services and resources be maintained? If so, at what cost? To whom? Where will the expressive arts figure in the priorities of a governing body hell-bent on efficiency and accountability? There is a real danger that educational philosophies evolved over a period of time and shared between professionals in the schools and the LEA Advisory Services could be displaced by the whim or passion of ephemeral fashion promoted by amateurs, probably in the name of economy.

To recognise that such difficulties can arise should not be interpreted as pessimism or as a mild form of fatalistic resignation. Rather, these possibilities should serve to emphasise the urgency of the present situation if the case for the expressive arts is to be imaginatively and convincingly presented, irresistible momentum generated, and expenditure patterns established within the limited time available. For too long expressive arts teachers have assumed defensive roles. The need now is for positive and confident action based on a careful analysis of the main issues involved, and the formulation of strategies underpinned with sound philosophy. There has not been such a drastic rethinking of the curriculum in recent times. The arts teacher can sigificantly influence this process, even within the constraints imposed by the Government.

To do this will require more than the reiteration of yesterday's arguments. Times have changed – often quite literally, both in terms of the shape of the school day, with an increasing number of schools experimenting with the Continental pattern, and through the introduction of the teachers' contract of 1,265 hours. Such changes demand a reappraisal of the balance between curricular and extra-curricular provision. Similarly, arts education will need to be seen against a broader context than that of terminal education which dies a death when the pupil reaches the age of 16. Increasingly the boundaries between school and community are being dismantled and the process is likely to be accelerated in the years ahead. The case of expenditure on the arts may be more plausible where there is a community dimension.

Four themes ahead

If the opportunity for development is to be seized, there are four themes in particular which need urgent consideration:

a) In the light of comments made earlier in this chapter it is important to ensure that there is a shared definition of what is meant by arts education. In particular it is necessary to distinguish the *educational* function of the arts from the *social* function. It is also important for there to be an understanding of the creative process.

Who needs to understand? It would help, perhaps, to begin with the expressive arts teachers, for unless there is dialogue it is not possible to share views and interpretations. But the real need is to provide guidance (and training?) for parents and governors. They cannot manage well that which they do not understand.

b) The expressive arts should be viewed and treated as a generic group of disciplines, both by expressive arts teachers themselves and by administrators. Considerable strides have already been made in this direction, but there remain pockets of resistance where teachers nervously fear an erosion of territory or a dilution of standards. Schools are now required to produce short-term and medium-term curriculum development plans. Despite an outward appearance of rigidity (as implied by subject labels), there is reason to believe that the curriculum will become increasingly fluid. It is clear from attainment targets already produced for core subjects that some targets may be approached by a variety of routes and it is likely that the same broad principle will apply across the expressive arts. But of far greater importance than action based on inspired speculation is the need to provide *coherence* for this 'essential area of experience'.

c) A period of change must be accompanied by an appropriate in-service training programme if the changes are to be implemented smoothly and effectively. Some needs will no doubt be provided for centrally, at the instigation of Central Government or the LEA. Other needs will be local and may require a bespoke response. Every effort should be made to achieve a match between a school's *curriculum development* plans and its *professional development* programme.

d) With the advent of the local management of schools it will be desirable for each school to have a *policy for the expressive arts*. Without such a policy how is it possible to administer finances sensibly and creatively? It is also incumbent upon expressive arts teachers to make their collective voices heard during the designing of that policy. There is no other way of ensuring that their case has been fairly and adequately presented.

It is a major purpose of the succeeding chapters to discuss these four themes and other issues in some detail, partly to inform, partly to prompt the reader's own responses, and on occasions to suggest directions in which developments might profitably proceed. Above all, expressive arts teachers must cultivate a strong contempt for the impossible coupled with a determination to take full advantage of the opportunities presented within a changing scene.

CHAPTER 2 THE CASE FOR THE ARTS

'The arts – do we need them?'

Why is the question being asked? Is it to promote discussion and debate, or is to to tease and provoke mischief?

Who is the questioner? Is it an arts teacher examining, or re-examining, the basic philosophical foundations of his or her work – a self-analysis, perhaps reflecting a bruised ego or crushed morale caused by uncongenial working conditions and prompting the teacher to ask 'Why do I believe the arts are so important?'? Is it a school governor scrutinising the accounts in search of an area in which economies can be made? Is it a head faced with troublesome timetabling decisions or the need to reduce staff in a falling-rolls situation?

Of course one might easily extend the list of questioners to include parents, pupils, teachers in non-arts disciplines, employers, and politicians. The problem is that each questioner is really looking for a different type of answer, and a wide range of responses is not feasible in the space available here. Nevertheless, the reader will no doubt be able to draw from this chapter according to his or her needs.

Sense and sensibility

In the simplest terms education is 'about' helping pupils to make sense of the world around them (in all its aspects) and, in particular, it is 'about' equipping them with the tools to 'find' themselves in that world. To do this the school curriculum has traditionally been divided into subject areas, each providing a body of information comprising accumulated facts, opinions and concepts. Collectively these volumes of information supply the knowledge and establish the base camp for the pupils' adventure. But increasingly educationalists have come to appreciate that information alone is not enough, reason is not enough, and that true knowledge can best be acquired through experience. Modern curriculum developments have sought ways of adding an experiential dimension to the learning process, thus deepening and enriching understanding.

A characteristic feature of experience is that it is almost invariably acquired via the senses. We see, we hear, we taste, we feel for ourselves and therefore we *know*. Frequently what we experience cannot be communicated in words, nor in mathematical symbols, nor can it be subjected to laboratory tests for scientific proof, yet we know it to be true. Our senses are the antennae through which we experience and respond to nature, to relationships with others, to the environment, to members of other cultures, to art forms and to a myriad of happenings which occur during the course of our daily lives. From such experiences, ranging from the dramatic to the subtle and the subconscious, we each collate our own bank of 'knowledge' which in turn establishes our belief patterns and determines our behaviour.

If the senses are so essential as channels for consciousness and for experiences, it follows that the education of the senses must comprise an important element within any balanced curriculum. And with the education of the senses, we must associate increased awareness and attention to the range of experiences offered to the pupil within both the taught and the hidden curriculum.

How are the senses educated? How is awareness increased? Without doubt, initially in the company of others whose judgement is respected – and preferably whose enthusiasm is infectious! I recall an occasion a few years ago when my wife and I were holidaying in Scotland. Near to where we were staying there was a small loch, about nine kilometres in circumference. Tempted by the beautiful setting, at the earliest opportunity we walked around the loch, in no great haste, absorbing as far as we were able the many and varied facets of the scenery. A few days later we returned along exactly the same walk in the company of a local naturalist. The difference between the two experiences almost defies description. Now we saw the narrow vertical path on the trunk of the pine along which, for decades, generations of ants had busily made their way to the topmost branches in search of food; now we learned to identify the ageing tree by its balding crown; now, some distance from the path, we were able to recognise a rare orchid, and a butterfly seldom seen outside Scotland. Individual threads of sound were drawn from the tapestry of bird-song, the characteristic melodic and rhythmic patterns expertly analysed, and the performers identified. The experience was total. We had been taught how to see, how to listen, how to smell and, in consequence, we were more alive to the environment. Our understanding was more complete. In a short time the intelligence of our senses, our sensibility, had been educated, just as surely as mathematical or scientific intelligence might be educated in the classroom or the laboratory.

The heightening of awareness and the fine-tuning of the senses is not, of course, the prerogative of any particular discipline or group of disciplines and one would hope that experiential learning occurs in school throughout the curriculum at all ages and, indeed, throughout life. The point is that awareness is focused according to personal predisposition and according to what is being looked for, often to the exclusion of other aspects. It would have been interesting, for instance, to have repeated that walk around the loch in the company of, let us say, an artist, or a land developer, or a freshwater biologist, or a geologist. We see the world according to the eyes we are wearing at any given time.

Frequently there is an urgent desire to freeze, to record, to give permanence to the experience received via the sensory antennae. Its significance is instantly recognised and there is a need both to explore the experience and to 'file' it for future reference. On these occasions the type of experiential (and sometimes intuitive) knowledge gained may be incapable of being reduced to straight discursive statements. The need is to find a vocabulary, a symbol system, appropriate to the task. Eisner summarises the situation thus: *'Each symbol system – maths, the sciences, art, music, literature, poetry and the like – functions as a means for both the conceptualisation of ideas about aspects of reality and as a means for conveying what one knows to others. Each symbol system has unique capabilities. Each symbol system sets parameters upon what can be conceived and what can be expressed'*.

This last sentence is of paramount importance. It is essential that the capabilities and limitations of the various symbol systems are identified and respected, and that the contributions they are able to make within the educational process are seen not to compete with but to complement each other. The arts, in their distinctive ways, do provide access to an area of 'knowledge' unreachable by any other means. *The arts do provide another way of knowing.*

The arts also provide the means by which that experiential knowledge can be communicated to, and shared with, others. In order to be used, and in order to be expressed, the experience needs to be given what Ross calls *'a stabilising structure'*, a form of expression publicly understood. Once encapsulated in such a form, the experience can be explored, distilled, refined and illuminated. In the mind of the creator it will connect with other similar experiences as gradually the creative process evolves towards the finished art piece. Acquiring the facility to communicate in this way is not easy, but without that facility the individual is cut off not only from an external area of experience and knowledge but also from a world within him/herself.

That external realm includes the works of others, the great and the not so great, the historical and the contemporary, and those who give expression to a different culture whether it be ethnic or social. The world within is one greatly dominated by images, mostly visual or audio. We conceptualise in images, we imagine in images – as the very word implies – before we clad those concepts or ideas with words. And our capacity to exercise these processes is as surely dependent upon the acquisition of a wide and practised image vocabulary as verbal reasoning is dependent upon word vocabulary. To lack ability in either is a handicap likely to affect both personal experience and personal growth. Images in the mind have no edges. They are confined only by the rational limitations we impose, and by the range and flexibility of the image vocabulary we have at our command.

The expressive disciplines

It is not by accident that the creative arts are referred to as the expressive disciplines. That they are expressive is self-evident, but the demands in terms of discipline and rigour are frequently underestimated and failure to produce the desired standard in performance or representation is often wrongly attributed to lack of talent. (Unfortunately, in the past, there have also been too many instances where arts teachers themselves have contributed to, if not created, the 'no talent' label which the individual has then carried for life.) There is no mystique. At one end of the creative spectrum we find a small number of geniuses and at the other end a corresponding minority who seem to be devoid of any aesthetic sensibility. But, by definition, the majority have some place on the continuum between the two extremes. By far the greatest inhibitors of the development of creative and expressive abilities are (a) social attitudes and (b) absence of sustained effort and persistence.

Social attitudes are powerful and are often entrenched, stubborn and difficult to change. They may well be built on foundations which are unreliable, perhaps innocently depending upon misinformation, false assumptions, prejudice, ignorance or, quite frequently, outdated and irrelevant personal experience (what might be described as the 'Well, when I was at school ...' syndrome). Patterns of belief are formed which are 'comfortable' in that once they have been established they require little further thought. The stereotyped response is always to hand. By definition social attitudes reflect mass, rather than discriminating, opinion and offer a constant echo-chamber in which niggling personal doubts may reverberate, perhaps becoming exaggerated and distorted, and ultimately may contribute to the body of evidence representing the popular view. In the world of the pupil the defenders of such attitudes are frequently parents and other respected adults (often including non-expressive arts teachers) and, of course, peers. The pressures are considerable.

Regarding the second point – relating to sustained effort and persistence – I am persuaded that there are few other areas in education where problem-solving skills are so constantly exercised as in the expressive disciplines. Confronted with the blank sheet of paper, the primed canvas, the empty manuscript page or the ball of clay, the creative artist has a problem! Indeed one choice has already been made, since he or she has determined the medium most appropriate for what he or she has to express. But the process is just begun and from here until the completion of the work there will be a continuous stream of questions to be answered and decisions to be made. The demands in terms of persistence and concentration are considerable, and there are those who fall by the wayside, not through lack of ability but through a reluctance to take on the challenge.

Skills and attitudes

So what are the skills and attitudes associated with the creative process in the expressive arts? We might well include the following:

- observation/awareness of stimuli of any kind (e.g. visual, aural, tactile, kinaesthetic, social);
- ability to connect with other experiences;
- imagination;
- inventiveness/creativity;
- ability to produce divergent responses;

- ability to analyse, understand and recreate;
- decision making/problem solving;
- ability to select from a range of alternatives;
- concentration;
- persistence/'stickability';
- pursuit of quality;
- motor skills – coordination and control;

and we might well add:

- the ability to work with others or alone;
- the ability to listen;
- the ability to communicate;
- the ability to accept and use constructive advice.

It will immediately be apparent that none of these skills and attitudes is specifically confined to the arts. All can be improved, several can be acquired through sheer application and persistence, and most are transferable.

Can creativity be taught? Can it be improved? I am not sure that creativity can be taught where no seed obviously exists, for it is in this area of innate aptitude and creative fertility that the natural curve of distribution has some significance. But I have no doubt that performance can be improved. The gestation of a creative idea has three phases – the stimulus; the production of a wide range of possible responses; the recognition and selection of the response which appears to have the greatest appropriate potential – and in the educational context the teacher has a significant role to play in each phase. In the first phase he or she is usually responsible for the choice of stimulus and for the quality and quantity of the initial creative energy and motivation it will generate. In the second phase the teacher's particular responsibility is to provide a positive atmosphere in which even the most seemingly fanciful of suggestions has the possibility of incubation. The greatest impediment to the flow of imaginative ideas is the negative or lukewarm response, or even the dismissive 'Don't be silly'. Unfortunately many youngsters do live their lives in family environments where the preoccupation is with the 'harsh realities of the world as seen on TV', and where childhood fantasy and play are rarely shared or encouraged. It is not surprising that such children, deprived of a supportive and understanding audience in the home, cultivate a reticence and loss of confidence, even a genuine loss of belief in their own capabilities. It is a challenge to the teacher to provide compensatory support and to release potential wherever it may lie. There is a lot of it around and I am suggesting that most, if not all, children have within them more creative capacity than they themselves appreciate.

The third phase – the selection of a particular response which demonstrates, or seems to offer, the desired potential – is the most difficult. Recognising potential, as distinct from assessing an idea in its present state, is never easy and is perhaps a skill more readily acquired through mimesis and experience than by following arid guidelines.

I shall return to this theme in the next chapter, but for the moment it is my purpose merely to establish that the ability to be creative is not the prerogative of an élite minority, whether we are considering the arts or any other area of human endeavour. It is also my concern to reaffirm that the arts offer valuable channels of expression and communication, accessible to all, though I readily accept that not all art forms will be equally congenial to all people. By acknowledging this fact I am recognising that, for some, dance may be a more natural medium for expression than painting, whilst others may feel more at home with drama than with music.

But beyond the education of the senses and the acquisition of facilitating skills, the arts are concerned with a further dimension which involves:

- aesthetic awareness;
- self-awareness;
- the structured expression of feeling;
- the determining of values;
- the opportunity for individual expression and personal growth.

It is significant that the word 'awareness' appears once more, and I am tempted to suggest that it is the most important word in the arts vocabulary. Eisner, speaking of the experience that is latent in the sensory events that constitute the world, says: *'We must learn how to have such experiences. Even among things natural, trees, mountains, landscapes and the like, qualities do not speak for themselves. One must bring to them, as it were, a receptive attitude and an enquiring mind. One must ask to receive'.* But sensory awareness takes us only so far. Awareness of the response within is necessary to balance the equation.

Aesthetic awareness

In the case of aesthetic awareness, the unity between form and content, combined with coherence and elegance of expression, may evoke an echo within us which, in some strange way, can simultaneously both excite and calm. In the physical world it seems possible to identify a range of phenomena – including sunsets, rainbows and various scenes of outstanding beauty – which have universal appeal. Yet acknowledgement of the aesthetic qualities of an art work, or even of a natural object or landscape, need not necessarily be the result of a positive feeling response towards that object or view, for it is possible to appreciate the aesthetic properties of an object without warming to, or being attracted by, the object in question. For instance, it is possible to acknowledge the aesthetic qualities of a Bach fugue or a Chopin *étude* without otherwise responding positively to either. On the other hand, to create a work of art devoid of feeling content is a contradiction in terms. Similarly, to create a work of art devoid of aesthetic qualities is not possible. What distinguishes the purely aesthetic from the artistic is the *feeling* content contained in the latter. Not infrequently, one meets examples of contemporary design which exhibit aesthetic qualities resulting from an intellectual rather than a feeling response to a brief and which evoke an intellectual rather than a feeling response from the viewer. Where the balance tilts exaggeratedly away from the feeling response, the validity of the piece as an art work must be questioned. In short, it is possible to have the aesthetic without the artistic, but it is not possible to have the artistic without the aesthetic.

Aesthetic awareness is again, I suspect, cultivated rather than taught, and is acquired by osmosis rather than by instruction. During the formative stages in education much will depend upon the ambience of the environment, the selection and character of the models of excellence made available to the pupil and on the inspirational qualities and artistic taste of the teacher. Whilst it is possible to itemise the traditionally accepted criteria relating to aesthetic expectations in a particular art form in a given period of time, there is invariably scope to accommodate a range of opinions and interpretations, and personal preference will be determined by the unique mixture of experience, education and other fortuitous circumstances which have shaped the individual.

Self-awareness

If for no other reason, self-awareness is important because it offers, and implies, a degree of self-control. Until we are aware, there is no opportunity for deeper involvement and no opportunity for improvement, whatever aspect of our lives we may be considering. Much of our daily lives, and our interaction with others, is affected by a fairly direct response to the messages received via the sensory antennae referred to earlier. The demands of my inherited culture consciousness dictate that if I meet a stranger it is important to me that I am able to establish rapidly a position for that stranger within my own pattern of experience. I quickly assimilate, almost at a glance, such signals as sex, age, physical appearance and presence, dress and attitude, and speculatively make assumptions which are likely to influence my behaviour towards the stranger, at least until such time as my instincts have been confirmed or denied. The word 'instincts' is selected deliberately to indicate a combination of intuition and educated guess. How much of each is involved must depend largely on age and experience. In my case, as a mature adult, there is a wealth of experience to draw upon, but the young child faced with a stranger may feel fear or, at the other extreme, misplaced trust.

Sometimes rationality appears to play little part in determining behaviour – a perception which prompted Gibson to observe, *'Emotions are the key to most of what happens in our classrooms and schools'.* (Teachers would do well to ponder the question, 'What does it feel like to be a pupil in my classroom?' for there is no doubt that how the pupil *feels* will greatly influence how he or she will *behave.*) And, of course, we can all cite scores of instances when our actions have seemingly been determined by feeling rather than by reason. But closer analysis will show that many of these 'spontaneous' emotional reactions have been triggered and informed by previous experience absorbed into the subconscious, and that a whole series of decisions will have been made instantaneously and unconsciously to produce particular behavioural responses – just as in my supposed encounter with the stranger. Emotional responses are complex happenings and I have no intention of wandering into the preserve of the psychologist. I merely wish to recognise the tremendous energy generated by the emotions, and the fact that such energy provides a far stronger driving force for action than intellectual knowledge alone.

Abbs has commented that: *'A rational proposition can only materialise as action where there is fitting emotion. Emotion gives knowledge motion'*. Such a potent force is available to be used or abused, and the education of the emotions, the education of feeling, is essential if the individual is to be responsible for his or her actions and behaviour, and realise and express his or her full potential. It is a natural function of the arts to provide both the nourishment and opportunity for this development process.

If we depend on real-life experiences alone to provide the reservoir from which we can draw, we shall be restricted indeed. Life is too short, and our experiences will be confined to that very small, though important, world with which we make daily contact. Through an art work we are invited to share another perspective. The feeling world of the artist communicates with and involves our own feeling world, whether the medium be music, words, painting, dance or whatever. And through that dialogue our own vision is extended, our own awareness and sensibility enriched.

Perhaps the most obvious example of 'extended' experience in popular form exists in the television soap opera where, consciously or unconsciously, viewers identify with particular characters through some recognisable affinity with their own world and then, by sharing in the vicissitudes of those characters, are able to be transported into other situations they can feelingly imagine. At each twist and turn in the storyline there is an opportunity for the individual to ponder how he or she would react in the given circumstances – an opportunity for self-awareness, an opportunity for examining and questioning personal values.

In the works of great artists the focus is keen, the awareness is three-dimensional and the vision penetrating. Thus the theme of ambition as addressed in *Macbeth* searches into every dark corner of our own feelings, and through our sympathies, understandings and revulsions with happenings in the play we emerge knowing ourselves a little better. A universal truth has been illuminated. Our sensibility has been refined.

All art works conspire to increase the emotional vocabulary and to expand our feeling world into new territory. The feelings initially evoked in me when listening to the slow movement of Elgar's Cello Concerto may be reminiscent of similar feelings experienced at a time of great personal sadness. Certainly the emotional reservoir from which the experience is drawn seems to be the same. But then the Elgar movement expresses a different intensity, and the elaboration and development of the original ideas and mood somehow seem to ennoble my first response and introduce me to a 'new' range of feelings I was not previously aware that I possessed.

In their capacity to explore in such depth a closely focused and tightly defined range of feeling, individual art works often exceed the capabilities of comparable real situations in the quality of response aroused. A Wilfred Owen poem or a painting by a war artist can more potently convey the true horror and obscene carnage of the First World War than will thirty metres of newsreel film. What is more, the impact is likely to be sustained over a longer period. An art work offers opportunity for comment, empathy and reflection.

Of course, the arts are not alone in contributing to the emotional vocabulary – and indeed my plea is that all subject disciplines should seek ways of increasing the opportunities for experiential learning. It is simply the case that since they are primarily concerned with the feeling mode, the expressive arts are ideally placed to provide a considered programme for the education of the emotions, for the education of feeling.

In this educational process, my first concern is that pupils should be encouraged to acknowledge that they have feelings. My second concern is that they should be encouraged to identify, and more precisely examine, those feelings. These may seem to be modest requests but there is ample evidence to suggest that for some pupils there may be difficulties. There are households in which expressions of feelings are most certainly not encouraged, and displays of emotion positively discouraged, as are indications of affection: households in which, for example, it is unacceptable for the young male to exhibit feelings of tenderness. Such negative, suppressive attitudes and gender stereotyping are deeply ingrained by the time the child enters formal education, and teachers are left with the task of resuscitating an emotionally dessicated youngster.

To enable the healthy development of an individual to take place, whether child or adult, there must be self-awareness of all shades of emotional response, pleasant and unpleasant, and awareness too of the conditions and causes which evoke those responses – issues, concerns, curiosities, situations, objects (natural and man-made), attitudes and relationships. Only then can that individual observe him/herself, as it were, from a distance. Only then can he or she explore alternative forms of expression or behaviour.

The structured expression of feeling
What are the alternative outlets available? Witkin has conveniently provided two labels which we will borrow to polarise in an exaggerated way two broad categories of emotional response. They are the 'reactive' and the 'reflexive'.

'Reactive' behaviour occurs when the individual is concerned merely with releasing pent-up emotional energy, whatever the source may be – joy, excitement, sadness, anger or revenge. In its anti-social form the emotion, unrefined and unbridled, may find expression in wanton vandalism, violence, loss of temper or tantrums. The preoccupation is with the discharge of energy, giving vent to feelings, often regardless of any damage caused either to property or people. The desired reduction of tension may have been achieved but in all other respects such behaviour is negative, on occasions leaving the 'actor' with a chain of consequences as unwelcome as the initial cause. In addition, little will have been learned from the experience and there is every likelihood that the pattern will be repeated.

'Reflexive' behaviour refers to a response in which the individual contains his or her emotional response and, instead of an explosive outburst, channels the emotional charge through a structured expressive form, i.e. through a work of art, either in its creation or its performance. In contrast with the 'reactive' response, 'reflexive' behaviour is positive, enabling the 'actor' to work through, and become aware of, his or her feelings whilst at the same time providing a medium through which those feelings, in controlled and perhaps more eloquent terms, may be communicated to others.

The beneficial effects on the individual of the 'reflexive' alternative are self-evident, but it is not always appreciated that, as a society, we cannot afford to neglect the education of the emotions. We do so at our peril. We live in difficult times, when the figures for violent crime seem to be constantly rising. The political response is to create a larger police force and to advocate tougher sentences for offenders. All, one might add, with limited success. Maybe, for once, the politicians could learn from the world of education, for there is abundant evidence to demonstrate that schools which attach importance to the expressive arts have, in general, fewer discipline problems than schools with similar intake but in which the expressive arts are of little or marginal importance. I would suggest that there may be two reasons for this: (a) the opportunity for 'reflexive' expression referred to above, and (b) the nature of the relationship between teacher and pupil established during the creative process. Expressive work demands recognition of, and respect for, each pupil's individuality, and the extent to which the child will reveal the very private inner world is directly related to the level of trust placed in the teacher. These twin elements of respect and trust produce a climate in which self-discipline thrives.

It seems appropriate to note as a rider that if the expressive arts contribute significantly to the education of the emotions, there is a need for more rather than less involvement during the years of adolescence, a period of considerable emotional turmoil for most teenagers. It also seems appropriate to observe that there is no known curve of distribution for feeling. And certainly there is no correlation between feelings and intelligence. The arts must be for *all*.

The determining of values

As educationalists we must be sensitively aware of the cultural environment in which these adolescents are spending their 'troubled' years. The verbal culture of the nineteenth century, with its references to historical events and Christian heritage, has given way to a visual and audio culture with a distinctly contemporary flavour and with scarcely a glance back to the past. The opportunity for reflection, offered by the verbal tradition, has been replaced by a demand for instant recognition or understanding accompanied by an apparent desire for a continuous stream of visual and/or aural stimuli – a continuity which precludes reflection and which may on the one hand trivialise or, on the other hand, consign experiences to the subconscious, undigested. Modern technology, in the form of the video recorder and the personal stereo, has extended facilities for continuous viewing and listening. At the same time, the Church can no longer claim to be the single most significant influence in our culture. That position has been claimed by television, and the clichés of the pulpit have been brushed aside by the clichés of the soap opera and the entertaining jingles of the commercial break.

From our immediate cultural environment we acquire sets of values relating to taste, morals, codes of behaviour, attitudes towards material possessions, and so on. Many of the influences which shape such attitudes take hold through the imitation of others and through imbibing their attitudes and standards unconsciously. For many teenagers that cultural environment is dominated by television – a singularly surreptitious force. It was the power of mass culture, and of television in particular, which caused Abbs to comment: *'If, under the influence of the school, the adolescent's rational knowledge about the world is being slowly extended, we must realise at the same time that his emotional attitudes to life are being shaped by another pressure, a force alien to the sober routine of school, and possessing greater energy in that it appeals, however crudely, to the irrational level of the human mind'.*

It is not my purpose to be unfairly critical of television – there are, of course, very many fine programmes produced to satisfy a variety of tastes – but it is my purpose to insist that we have an obligation to see that pupils leave school visually and aurally literate as well as verbally literate. The awareness skills, referred to frequently in this chapter, are as applicable to images and sounds created and communicated by humans as to those which occur in the natural environment. In particular there is a need to understand the ways in which humans can manipulate images and sound for good or ill. There is also a need to identify visual and aural metaphors and to become discerning in the face of the anaesthetising wash of mass-media images – both visual and aural. The power of such people as the television advertiser or the documentary film producer is being increasingly recognised and, perhaps in some instances, motives may be examined with a degree of suspicion. But scepticism, belligerence and obstinacy are inappropriate tools with which to face the modern television professional. There is no substitute for familiarisation with the practical processes of film-making for enhancing true understanding and appreciation. Involvement in discussions relating to the varying impacts of images produced by selected camera angles, lighting arrangements, choice of sound track and so on slowly but surely equips the individual with an expanding technical knowledge of the medium and enables him or her to be more acutely aware of the interpretations of the subject matter. By such means is visual literacy made possible.

In a not dissimilar way there is a clear need for aural awareness and aural literacy. We live in an age when silence is a rare commodity. In many homes the waking hours are continually accompanied by either the radio or the stereo or the television. Outside the home we have become accustomed to the relaxing music of the department store, the restaurant and the supermarket, or even the sudden raucous intrusion of an untamed 'ghetto blaster' disturbing an erstwhile peaceful atmosphere. Amplified sound has become one of the characteristic features of our times and we sometimes fail to appreciate that the spread of technological advance has in many ways outpaced the development of an understanding of how to use the facility most effectively. An almost inevitable consequence of this fact is that the more we hear the less we listen, and so fail to discriminate between the good, the bad and the indifferent – between the true, the false and the misleading or mischievous.

We can divide aural awareness into three progressive stages: (a) an awareness of progressive sound images; (b) the ability to focus on those images; and (c) the testing of the validity of the images in terms of their effectiveness and appropriateness in the particular context. The three-stage process holds good whether we are considering music or similar sound patterns, theatrical dialogue, discursive argument or even everyday conversation. Competence in aural awareness graduates into aural literacy and encourages the listener to become increasingly quality-conscious and selective.

Of course, visual and aural literacy benefit not only the individual but also society as a whole. The individual is enriched by acquiring skills which enable him or her to be more consciously aware of his or her environment, and society benefits for exactly the same reason. For if an increasing number of individuals become more aesthetically aware, there will inevitably be some expression of their attitudes in the environment they help to create – even if, for some, that influence extends little further than the home. We are educating young people to become guardians of the quality of life – for our generation, for their own, and for generations to come.

The opportunity for individual expression and personal growth

At this point it may be helpful to draw together the various threads of the discussion thus far and to express them diagramatically:

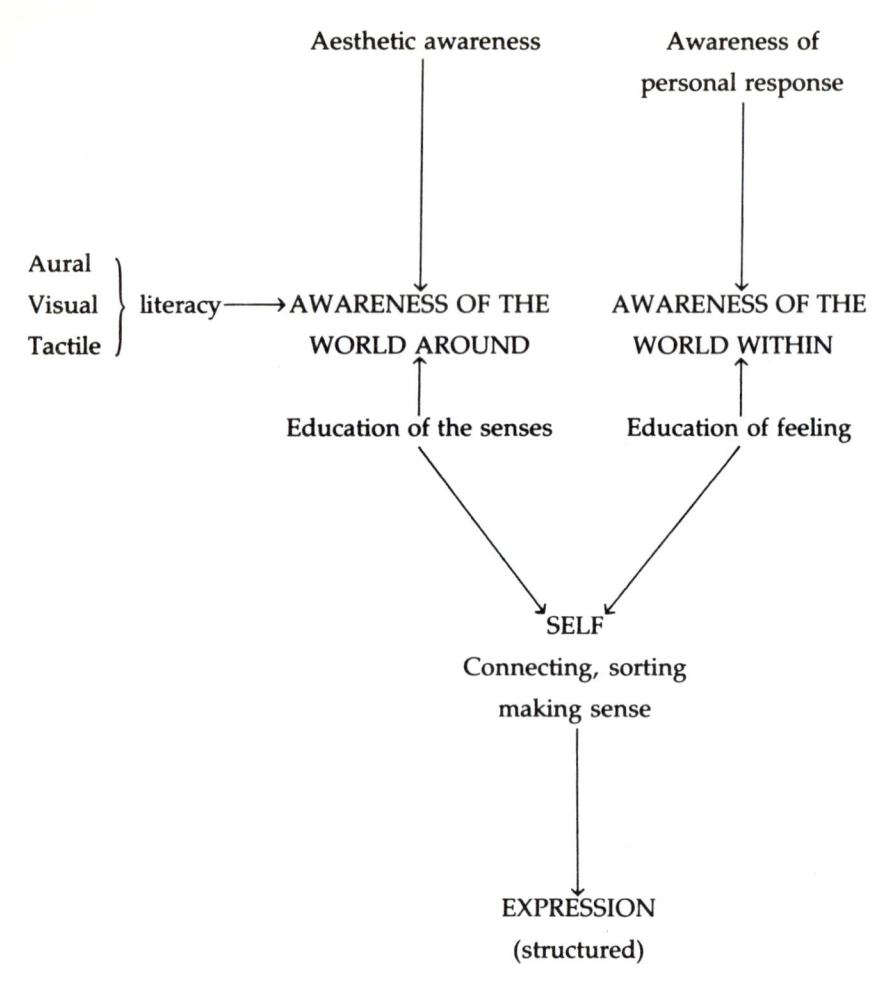

```
                    Aesthetic awareness        Awareness of
                            |                  personal response
                            |                       |
                            |                       |
Aural  ⎫                    ↓                       ↓
Visual ⎬ literacy ⟶ AWARENESS OF THE        AWARENESS OF THE
Tactile⎭              WORLD AROUND             WORLD WITHIN
                            ↑                       ↑
                            |                       |
                    Education of the senses   Education of feeling
                             \                      /
                              \                    /
                               \                  /
                                ↘   SELF   ↙
                              Connecting, sorting
                                making sense
                                      |
                                      |
                                      ↓
                                 EXPRESSION
                                  (structured)
```

The diagram is by now self-explanatory, but it is worth repeating that the areas of knowledge and experience explored during the process it represents are most accessible – often *only* accessible – through the expressive arts. The arts offer coherence to an otherwise disparate collection of sensuous and affective responses. The significance of such a contribution to a balanced educational programme (i.e. the curriculum) has been well identified by Robert Witkin: *'There is a world that exists beyond the individual, a world that exists whether or not he exists. The child needs to know about this world, to move in it and manage himself in it. The curricula of our secondary schools are filled with this world. Everywhere the child turns he encounters it in the brute facts of history, chemistry, mathematics, and so forth. There is another world, however, a world that exists only because the individual exists. It is the world of his own sensations and feelings. He shares the former world with others. He moves around it with them, for it is a world of facts, of public space and "objects". He shares the second world with no one. It is the world of private space and of the solitary subject . . . . If the price of finding onself in the world is that of losing the world in oneself, then the price is more than anyone can afford'.*

The arts and the economy

Whilst the educational case for the arts is strong, there have always been critics – perhaps particularly in political circles – who have considered the arts to be a luxury the nation could well do without. The arts have been accorded the reputation of being non-viable and continually in need of vast subsidies from the Arts Council. For such critics, the report on 'The Economic Importance of the Arts in Britain' published in July 1988 by the highly respected Policy Studies Institute must have been a huge disappointment. For example, the researchers discovered that the arts directly employ 2% of the employed population; in 1985–6 the turnover amounted to 2.5% of all spending, and was comparable in size to the market for motor vehicles; the arts produce 3% of British export earnings, and more invisible exports than either civil aviation or insurance; on average they generate a quarter of the country's earnings from tourism.

Maybe the comparatively trifling amount spent on subsidies is not such a bad investment! Maybe the job prospects are not so restricted as one might have been led to believe – and certainly the range is very diverse. Maybe, even on economic grounds, the arts need to be taken seriously.

In conclusion

To conclude this chapter, it is appropriate to return to the educational argument and to leave the final word with the Gulbenkian Report: *'In looking at the value of any activities, we can distinguish at least two sorts: first, those that are absolutely worthwhile in themselves; second, those that are worthwhile only insofar as they help to bring these other things about. Many of the activities which are demanded as being basic elements of the school curriculum fall into this second class of value. They have an instrumental value in acquiring things that are valued in themselves. The activities of the arts fall into the first class. They are absolutely worth spending time on for the sake of satisfactions that are intrinsic to them'.*

CHAPTER 3 THE CREATIVE PROCESS AND THE ROLE OF THE TEACHER

An introduction to the process

Awareness, response, structured form. I can think of no more succinct way of defining the arts experience. The previous chapter considered each of these aspects in a variety of contexts. The purpose of this chapter will be to explore the creative process more fully – to apply the attitude of awareness to what goes on in the classroom – and to examine the changing role of the teacher as the process unfolds. At each stage the pupil's needs change and at various times the teacher may become instructor, drill sergeant, inspiration, expert, guru, midwife, confidant or audience. But perhaps the most helpful of these images is that of midwife. It is Peter Abbs who reminds us that Socrates saw his vocation as being *a midwife to other men's conceptions* and that seems to me to be a particularly apt role for the expressive arts teacher. A prime responsibility of the teacher must be to facilitate the safe delivery of the art work conceived by the pupil. An analysis of the evolution of an art work – which for want of a better description I am calling 'the creative process' – will perhaps help to identify a parallel analysis of the pupil's needs.

Let us begin by dividing the process into six stages (a detailed elaboration of the three phases referred to earlier). They are:

- preparation;
- inspiration/stimulus;
- gestation;
- growth;
- completion;
- evaluation.

Of course, in practice there is no way in which these stages are self-contained. For example, evaluation must be an ongoing process throughout the composition of an art work since at every point there are factors to be weighed, decisions to be taken and perhaps adjustments to be made. Nevertheless the main evaluation must occur at the end, when some assessment of the success or failure of the assignment will be made. Similarly, although the key stimulus will provide the initial reason for the work's creation, it may be necessary for the teacher to produce additional stimuli *en route* either to generate further new ideas or to illustrate alternative ways of using and organising material, possibly by reference to the works of established artists. However, despite fluidity of this nature throughout the process, the concept of the six-stage structure is a particularly helpful one, providing the pupil with a clear understanding of the unfolding developments, and offering the teacher a framework within which to chart the individual pupil's needs. Furthermore it is a process common to creative work in all art forms and, with suitable modifications, is appropriate for pupils of all ages and levels of ability.

Preparation

The period of preparation is concerned particularly with educating three strands of understanding which are in practice extricably interrelated but which, for the moment and for convenience, will be separated. They are medium, form, and vocabulary.

Whatever the medium chosen and whatever the learning programme may be, there must be an opportunity for the pupil to explore the medium, to indulge in a degree of sensory enjoyment and experiment, to savour naturally something of the medium's character. It is a sad fact that as the pupil progresses through our education system, less and less time is made available for experimentation – and pressure on time leads to an imposition of knowledge from without rather than personal discovery from within. I am not advocating chaos in the classroom. I am advocating a guided exploration of the medium which leads the pupil so far and then allows him or her to make his or her own discoveries: an exploration which opens up new vistas the pupil would otherwise probably never have found. Such a process generates a degree of novelty (and perhaps even excitement), ownership and experiential learning. It also provides the core for a 'medium vocabulary' – a vocabulary of what can and what cannot be expressed in the medium. As the pupil reflects further and more deeply on the specific qualities and uniqueness of the medium, so that vocabulary will become refined and expanded. The world around will be viewed with new eyes as the pupil becomes increasingly conscious of art works in the medium, and as he or she considers objects and experiences in terms of their suitability for expression in, or translation into, that medium.

'Hands-on' experience of the medium is, of course, not enough. The pupil will also need to become familiar with ways in which responses and ideas are normally organised and structured when working in that particular medium. With the assistance of the teacher he or she will need to become acquainted with such structural and compositional elements as balance, repetition and pattern, and may – at a suitable stage and in a suitable way – be introduced to such concepts and dynamics as rhythm, line, colour and movement. Whatever the pupil's age or ability level the shared first objectives should be (a) a basic grasp of forms appropriate to the medium, and (b) care in the selection of a form appropriate to the task in hand.

Acceptance of the conventions of the medium, at least during the early stages, is advised for a variety of reasons:

a) the conventions generally represent a synthesis of the accumulated experience of artists in the particular art form over a long period;

b) the pupil will be working in a 'public' art form, the elements of which are publicly understood;

c) innovation which totally ignores established criteria degenerates into chaos – there must be clear points of reference for innovation to be recognised for what it is;

d) the great innovators of the past have invariably first demonstrated their mastery over existing forms before opening up new paths.

At all times it is important for the young creative artist to have access to good examples of work by others, both established artists and other pupils. He or she should also be encouraged to collect his or her own 'anthology', whatever the medium. In addition to providing pleasure, such material will no doubt offer further opportunity for analysis and discussion, and may well serve as a source of inspiration for the generation of ideas. The notion of analysis may sound rather grand when referring to the art work of young pupils, but it is never too early to introduce the pupil to the need for a match between the chosen medium and the consequent form or forms a piece of art work might take, however simply that concept is presented.

The need to discuss leads quite naturally to the third strand –

vocabulary. But I would suggest that the young artist needs not one vocabulary but three: to enable him or her to discuss, to think, and to express. Whilst again they are interrelated, each is quite distinct in the function it is required to fulfil.

The impoverished vocabulary of the average adolescent when invited to comment on a work of art or on a performance piece is almost embarrassing to behold. It is likely that the work will be consigned to one of three categories: 'bril', 'all right', or 'rubbish'. An extravagantly emotional work might prompt the description 'nice'. The problem is that not only are such adjectives imprecise, they also discourage further discussion. They represent the final word on the subject without saying anything about the constituent elements which 'justify' the label.

But can it be that arts educators should share at least some of the responsibility for such 'succinct' evaluations? In order to communicate freely the pupil requires an adequate vocabulary, an understanding of how to use the vocabulary appropriately and effectively, and the opportunity for regular practice. The acquisition and fluent use of such a vocabulary can only be cultivated over a long period of time. It needs to be progressively nurtured and purposefully exercised.

The vocabulary can be assembled systematically, focusing on three different aspects:
a) a *technical* vocabulary – relating to form, elements of composition, and any specialist vocabulary associated with the particular medium, etc.;
b) a *descriptive* vocabulary – facilitating not only narrative description but also requiring a degree of analytical awareness relating to such features as style, character, mood, etc.;
c) a *qualitative* vocabulary – enabling the pupil to make specific, positive and appropriate evaluative comments regarding the effectiveness of a particular art work.

The development of the vocabulary cannot be left to chance, it must be taught. It is a responsibility of the teacher to equip the pupil with a vocabulary which will not only enable him or her to reflect and comment, but which will also provide a tool with which he or she may probe to a deeper understanding. It will therefore include terms and adjectives, as well as definitions of concepts. On occasions, it may stimulate expressions of private emotional response not common to everyday discourse. The content of the vocabulary should be discussed between the expressive arts teachers both to identify the very considerable areas of overlap and also to raise awareness of specific interpretations or varying shades of meaning in different disciplines.

The acquisition of such a vocabulary has little to do with age but everything to do with usage. The appropriate use of vocabulary should be expected, encouraged and acknowledged as a natural feature of communication whether in one-to-one dialogue between teacher and pupil or in group/class discussion.

There is considerable evidence to demonstrate that range and quality of vocabulary directly affect the capacity to think. We need words to provide the symbol system by which we can summarise and identify concepts. For example, the Hopis of North Arizona have no equivalent for our word 'time'. They are therefore unable to conceive time in our terms. However, they are able to comprehend a broad pattern dictated by the cycle of the seasons. Similarly, in his novel *Nineteen Eighty-Four*, George Orwell creates a new language, 'Newspeak', with a deliberately restricted vocabulary in order to restrict the thinking of the people of Oceania. Orwell writes: *'Newspeak was designed not to extend but to diminish the range of thought, and this purpose was indirectly assisted by cutting the choice of words down to a minimum'*.

The challenge to the expressive arts teacher is, of course, precisely the opposite – it is the challenge to provide a vocabulary which generates ideas and stimulates expression. The cultivation of a verbal vocabulary along the lines mentioned above will obviously assist the process, but that alone is not enough. The imagination needs nourishment, particularly sensory nourishment and experience, if it is to be enriched. It is often said that 'We are what we eat'. It has also been observed that 'We become what we experience'. Both clichés have some significance for the expressive arts teacher. A diet of Mills and Boon will never produce a Shakespeare. But conversely, by providing a stimulating environment – including access to exciting and imaginative resource materials as well as to inspiring art works – and through the exploration of many and varied ways of extending the pupil's range of experiences, the teacher can make available a whole new territory of 'thought'. He or she can provide the pupil with a non-verbal language, a vocabulary of experience, which is capable of erupting and bubbling into an art work, at which point – in order to enjoy permanence and meaning – feeling, experience and ideas need to find expression in structured form, verbal or otherwise.

But there are other 'vocabularies' which expand or constrain thought. The following anecdote will perhaps illustrate the point. A few years ago, when Craft, Design and Technology was much in fashion, I was well acquainted with the work of a teacher who had been trained some twenty years earlier as a woodwork teacher. He was a fine craftsman, and frequently paid tribute to the tutor of his student days whom he admired greatly. In particular he recalled that the tutor had instilled into his students that 'All the skills of a woodworker are demonstrated in the making of a box. If you can make a box, you can make anything!' Accordingly, generations of pupils had learned to make boxes, complete with immaculate dovetails or even hidden dovetails. Now, with the advent of CDT, his world was in disarray. Dovetails were 'out of the charts'. Problem solving had entered at Number One. The situation was further complicated by the fact that pupils – girls as well as boys! – were sometimes being encouraged to combine woodwork and metalwork in one artefact. Reluctantly accepting the challenge of the changing scene, the teacher attended numerous in-service training courses, determined to become an accomplished teacher of CDT. The extraordinary thing was that despite the good intentions, and despite the training, whatever brief he set his classes the results looked remarkably like boxes, made from wood, often with immaculate dovetail joints!

The message was clear – that over the years the teacher's own thinking had become stilted and cramped and primarily skill-orientated. The imagination had been made largely redundant, and now when it was required to work again, it produced the only response with which it felt comfortable. What is more, these same limitations were obviously influencing his teaching style and were therefore indirectly restricting the thinking capability of his pupils. Gradually, as the teacher regained his self-confidence, his own imaginative juices were revitalised and he became both enthused and excited by the seemingly endless range of opportunities now available both to him and to his pupils. He also began to experience the frustration caused by having access to only a limited range of skills, however polished, and so he introduced a much wider repertoire, including skills in which he himself had previously little or no personal expertise. In a short period of time the transformation in the work of his pupils was dramatic. Freed from the ubiquitous dovetail, and armed with a portfolio of varied skills, the pupils' imaginations were given air, emancipated, and their responses seldom disappointed. Above all else the evidence demonstrated the extent to which the range of skill vocabulary in any particular medium determines not only what can be expressed but what can be conceived.

The development of technical skills is frequently regarded as the single most important goal during the period of preparation. The purpose is clear – it is to promote confidence, competence and mastery in the handling of the medium, to facilitate thinking in the medium (as described above) and to enable the artist/pupil to express what he or she wants to express. With such clarity of purpose it may at first be surprising to learn that difficulties can exist. But exist they do, sometimes to the extent of 'turning-off' the very people such skill programmes are intended to help.

One area of difficulty is associated with the perceived relevance of any skill task when it is detached from its use or application. Like many of my contemporaries, I can claim that when I left school I was an expert in the construction of mortice and tenon joints, providing the material used was red deal and that each piece of wood measured 8 inches × 2 inches × 1 inch! I can also claim that the number I made would have qualified me for an entry in the *Guinness Book of Records* had it then been in existence. And yet I can recall no occasion when I was invited to apply that skill usefully. Although such an occurrence is less likely to happen now, the tension illustrated by the example still exists. The teacher knows that competency in a skill can only be acquired through rigour and, in some cases, drill. To perform well, the artist needs to be as disciplined as the athlete. But few pupils are motivated by the 'because it's good for you' argument. They tire of becoming perpetual travellers and want, sometime, to arrive.

There is a fine balance between stretching pupils to maximise their potential and overstretching them to the point where they want no more of it. An over-zealous desire for accuracy can be self-defeating. There have been 'great' artists who were not particularly adept at producing accurate likenesses, and it is not uncommon to meet musicians who experience difficulty in singing in tune. And yet high competency in such skills tends, in many instances in education, to be prized far above other qualities. Ross speaks of the child reaching the *'representational crisis'*. Considerable sensitivity is required of the teacher to appreciate exactly how far each pupil can be taken. Not all pupils want to be expressive arts specialists and it is both futile and damaging to apply the same criteria across a wide range of ability.

This may sound ludicrously obvious, but the fact remains that by the upper years of the secondary phase the arts diet for the non-specialist is decidely meagre and unappetising. Failure to achieve specialist standards has left the pupil with nowhere to go. If and where such a situation arises, the school is failing the pupil. Let us recall that a characteristic feature of the arts experience is that it provides access to 'another way of knowing', to a world of experience and 'knowledge' unreachable by other means. It is therefore essential that if one route is blocked alternative paths must be offered. Yes, it is a problem. Without an appropriate range of skills, experience and the ability to express must be restricted, and yet insistence on too high a level of skill competency will also impede access to that experience.

A similar tension exists between the spontaneity of ideas and vitality of expression characteristic of childhood, and the demands for technical competency expected from adolescence onwards. Commenting on children's progress in drawing and the transition from primary to secondary school, Sheila Payne makes the point well: *'The new emphasis must seem a curious betrayal of values acquired in primary school where the immediacy of artistic statements may have won more approval. The resultant "culture shock" deprives many of the possibility of continuing their own development in drawing and of extending its enriching powers as well as its stimulus to their own thinking and learning'*.

The dilemma for the teacher is how to ensure that technical skills and conventions facilitate rather than inhibit and repress the expression of unspoiled originality. When the facilitating skills become more important than what is being said, there is clearly a need to question priorities. In an era when the preoccupation is with educational measurement and accountability, such an imbalance is easily reached, however inadvertently. To pursue Sheila Payne's point, in such a climate the child who in the primary school was artistically loquacious, may become tongue-tied and may ultimately prefer to remain dumb in the belief that no one is interested in *what* he or she has to say, merely in *how* he or she says it. Communication is primarily about wanting to be listened to.

To summarise, the truly effective teaching of creative skills can

only be achieved where there is a shared understanding between pupil and teacher on three points:
a) the specific purpose and relevance of the skills being learned and how they can be applied;
b) what is a realistic level of attainment for the pupil, and therefore what constitutes reasonable demand and expectation;
c) how soon there will be opportunity to apply the newly learned skills in a 'real' situation.

The period of preparation should aim to combine thoroughness with brevity. A marriage of the two generates purposeful activity and encourages a readiness to take on additional skills as the work proceeds and as need dictates.

Inspiration/stimulus

The preparation having been completed, the pupil is then 'available' for inspiration – for 'breathing in' and responding to the stimulus. In selecting a suitable stimulus the teacher will need to consider a number of points.
a) Clarity of purpose. What is he or she trying to achieve? Why? Often the first question is more easily and more satisfactorily answered than the second! There is also a strong case for inserting a second 'Why?' – implying 'Was the first answer a truly valid reason, or was it a superficial and dismissive reflex response given without much thought?'.
b) Is there a good match between the skills taught and the likely expressive demands of the stimulus?
c) What *experience* is the teacher attempting to explore in the pupil? Regrettably, it seems the question is seldom asked – and even when it is, it is not always answered.
d) Does the assignment have present significance as well as possible future promise?
e) Is it contributing to a coherent programme of learning?

The quality of the stimulus is the key to any piece of art work and the first essential characteristic of a good stimulus is its ability to radiate creative energy. The powerful stimulus will contain within it something which 'will out' – a charge, a dynamism, which evokes a feeling response, which generates expressive ideas and almost demands utterance. The process is affirmed by Robert Frost's comment, '*A poem begins as a lump in the throat . . .*' and by Wordsworth's definition of poetry as the '*spontaneous overflow of powerful feelings . . .* [which] *takes its origin from emotion recollected in tranquillity'*. Whilst it is true that the notion of emotional involvement will not be equally applicable to all stimuli, it is nevertheless a fact that the level of motivation is in every instance all-important. The quality of both process and product are likely to reflect directly the effectiveness of the stimulus and, by implication, the ability of the teacher to present the stimulus in an interesting and exciting manner.

To be effective the stimulus must have relevance, not only in the eyes of the teacher but also in the eyes of the pupil. Indeed, in terms of motivation what the teacher thinks matters little unless he or she is able to convince the pupil. This, of course, lies behind the persistent questioning 'Why?' referred to above. If the teacher has responded meaningfully and honestly to the question, and if he or she has taken into his or her reasoning the pupil's perspective, then there will be less likelihood of the pupil interjecting his or her own 'Why?' as an impediment to progress when the stimulus is presented. For the pupil, relevance means particularly that the stimulus connects with *his* or *her* world of experience. The more direct the connection, the stronger the motivation is likely to be. Conversely, the further away from direct experience the requirements of the stimulus are, the greater will be the need to 'justify' the selection and the weaker will be the radiated beams of creative energy.

The third prong in the effective presentation of stimulus material is clarity. It is not enough for the teacher to know what he or she wants. Those wishes or instructions must be communicated clearly and unambiguously to the pupils. Pupils must know exactly what is expected from them. They need to know the precise constraints within which the assignment is to be completed. Many of us have suffered at some time from the 'Draw what you like for homework' invitation, and know only too well how totally inadequate and unhelpful such a brief is. Great artists throughout history have regularly chosen to impose their own constraints where these have not been set from without by the conditions of a commission, or by particular local circumstances. Consider, for example, Bartok's 'Music for String Instruments, Percussion and Celesta', Britten's 'Serenade for Tenor, Horn, and Strings', Purcell's 'Fantasia on one note', Beckett's *Waiting for Godot*, or Picasso's various experiments with restricted palettes. A good stimulus will have defined parameters relating to such features as medium, palette range, scope, form and time. Obviously the specific constraints will vary enormously and will be selected as appropriate for the particular assignment. The point is that the constraints should be decided and stated at the beginning, not introduced or adjusted when the work is in progress. Often constraints serve to inspire rather than restrict.

It will also assist clarity of intent if the pupil has access to appropriate resource materials which illuminate or exemplify what is required – examples which challenge and generate additional ideas rather than imply or suggest answers.

Just as the presentation of the stimulus is prefaced by careful preparation, by both teacher and pupil in their different ways, so it should be followed by a 'breathing space', a deliberately staged period for reflection, during which the pupil has the opportunity to respond to, and become absorbed in, the various aspects and qualities of the stimulus. All too frequently a well-prepared stimulus with excellent potential is ruined by the conditions in which it is offered. Let me quote an example which may have a familiar ring to it.

It is decided that the city of York will provide an ideal stimulus for a class of 12-year-olds who are preparing a cross-curricular project involving both a humanities and arts approach. There are twenty-seven pupils in the class and much can be achieved during a day visit. The pupils already have a good background knowledge of the history of the city and the visit will be deliberately structured to provide first-hand experience of 'the feel' and atmosphere. Pupils and teachers discuss strategies for awareness and the various ways in which they might capture and express the experiences of the day. Then, in the next session they have together in school, the more expressive aspects of the project will begin in earnest. With detailed thought and planning the visit can indeed provide an excellent stimulus. The teacher duly approaches the headteacher to ask for permission to arrange the visit. 'What a very good idea!' says the head. 'I think you should take the whole year group. That will only be 150. You can squeeze them on three buses comfortably – possibly two if you try hard! But just one thing – do you think you could arrange it for the last week in term so that it doesn't disrupt their work?'

There is no need to comment on this scenario as it deteriorates from a selective educational visit to an outing for the masses – not to mention the hidden curriculum message associated with the timing of the event. Such absurdities and their implications are glaringly obvious at a distance, and yet on a smaller scale similar mistakes are perpetrated in many classrooms in most schools as a fairly regular occurrence – not deliberately, just through a failure to appreciate the need to give the stimulus 'air'. Purpose must be matched by opportunity if sensitivity of response is to be encouraged.

Gestation

The creative process is, of course, a seamless one and there is inevitably a considerable ebb and flow between the response to the stimulus and the generation of ideas which feed the structured expression of that response. The first stage will require the pupil to make connections between the stimulus and previous experience. The second stage will require him or her to explore and probe more closely, to seek a deeper, personal interpretation of the stimulus. It is rather like driving along the tourist route through mountainous scenery and arriving at a pull-in marked 'camera point'. From that spot there are beautiful panoramic views, and pictures are taken – but somehow, back home, those pictures often seem to lack 'magic'. Why? Probably because the camera point suited the communal perspective and provided the snapshot which said very little. The photographer needed to wander around, examine alternative perspectives and camera angles, perhaps focus in closely on specific features. Only then would he or she be in a position to consider alternative interpretations which would reflect a personal response. Then he or she could produce photographs rather than snapshots. In a similar way the pupil needs to find a personal perspective in response to the stimulus.

The gestation period is probably the most exciting and the most imaginative phase during the creative process, and is frequently the stage of deepest personal involvement. Having selected the personal perspective, now is the time for generating a flow of ideas and images (whatever the chosen medium might be). Now is the opportunity for examining 'What if?' alternatives, for compiling a 'sketch-book' collation of, for example, associated words, rhythms, graphic doodles and colours. It is a time for research, for referring to other source materials and for seeking examples of work by established artists in a related context or style. Gradually, particular ideas and images will become increasingly attractive and will seem to offer greater potential. These will obviously be examined and explored more carefully. But we might also note the observation of Jonathan Miller who reminds us that the best material can sometimes lie among the rejected ideas. He recalls that the breakthrough in the search for penicillin was discovered in the abandoned petri dish on the laboratory window-sill.

The role of the teacher throughout the gestation phase is a crucial one. Much will depend upon his or her capacity to respond sensitively to the needs of the individual pupil. This may mean acting as a sound-board; asking questions which lead the pupil to further ideas or areas of personal discovery; providing appropriate resource materials; introducing additional skills necessary for a specific purpose; and so on. It is a period during which the artist – and not only the young artist – feels particularly exposed, fragile and vulnerable. Private thoughts and responses are proffered, often coyly and half apologetically, for the attention and comment of the teacher, and a relationship of confidentiality and trust is established. The need to provide a positive and supportive atmosphere in which ideas can be generated and incubated – however 'unlikely' or fanciful they may seem – has already been stressed, and without this bond of mutual respect the creative process is considerably hampered. References have also been made to learning by mimesis or osmosis and it will be apparent that the teacher–pupil relationship outlined here encourages such a learning style. The tastes, methods of working and personal qualities of the teacher will inevitably permeate that relationship to a greater or lesser degree, perhaps in a way not commonly experienced in other subject disciplines.

Growth

By the end of the gestation period the artist will have sifted and teased a range of ideas, images and possible alternative interpretations, and a final selection will have been made. In some instances the artist may already have a clear vision of the completed work, but more frequently such a vision emerges only gradually during the period of growth, and even then may be subjected to various modifications. First the artist must select a form and style appropriate to what he or she has to express (and consonant with any constraints imposed by the brief for the assignment). Then he or she must develop the germinal ideas to give flesh and substance to the skeletal structure in a manner which illuminates the desired response to the stimulus and which invites or enables others to understand and to share that response.

The growth phase can be an extremely frustrating period for the pupil, since he or she will almost certainly at some point experience a feeling of inadequacy, an inability to express him/herself as he or she would wish. Imagination frequently outpaces technical skill, and personal limitations sometimes overshadow positive success. Creativity requires persistence, concentration and tenacity, and this stage in the process draws heavily upon the list of skills and attitudes presented in the previous chapter. Compared with the gestation phase, the artist needs perhaps to be less passionately involved and to be able to adopt a somewhat more distant stance. Those unacquainted with the demands of the creative process are sometimes sadly disillusioned to discover that the artist they imagined to be sitting in a studio or garret merely awaiting divine inspiration was, in fact, toiling long and tedious hours at his or her canvas, manuscript or whatever, perfecting, polishing or redrafting.

The responsibility of the teacher at this time is to make possible the safe delivery of the expressive response conceived by the pupil. (Almost inevitably, but unashamedly, one returns to the midwife image.) The teacher will be looked to for expert guidance, knowledge and inspiration, but above all for reassurance, encouragement, motivation and support. It is almost impossible to sustain persistence in a negative atmosphere of rejection and failure.

Completion

Perhaps the single most important point relating to the making of a piece of art work is knowing when to stop! This is a problem for the inexperienced artist in particular who will constantly seek to improve this or that, with the consequence that in a very short while the work loses its spontaneity and freshness, or its balance is destroyed. Comparatively few works have been spoiled as a result of understatement.

Once the work has been completed, it assumes a life of its own. In Louis Arnaud Reid's phrase, *'it becomes meaning-embodied'*, and others will bring to it and take from it according to their own needs and experiences. I recall a radio interview with Henry

Moore some years ago, and although I have no transcript of the programme the gist of what Moore had to say has remained clearly with me. It went something like this: A work of art is unique. In science it is likely that a discovery not made now will be made some time. It is always there for the unearthing. Had our generation not put a man on the moon, some later generation would have done so. Had Einstein not 'discovered' relativity, someone else would have. But no one else would ever have produced the paintings of Rembrandt, the plays of Shakespeare or the symphonies of Beethoven.

Of course each piece of art work the pupil produces will be to some degree unique, and on occasions when he or she has given all he or she has and the work is finished, there will be a residue, an indefinable feeling, a mingling of relief, satisfaction and proud ownership – not dissimilar from the mixture of feelings Rembrandt, Shakespeare and Beethoven no doubt experienced on the completion of their masterpieces!

Evaluation

The process of evaluation is, as I have suggested earlier, an ongoing one throughout the creation of an art piece. But the most important evaluation will take place when the work is completed. The life-circuit of an art work is not complete until there is an audience, however small. Abbs comments: *'If there was no one to view a Cezanne the painting would be devoid of aesthetic meaning for aesthetic meaning can only reside in the dynamic interaction between the work and the person looking ... The work exists in its action on the senses and imagination of the audience'*.

Whilst self-evaluation is an essential dimension of the creative process, because of personal emotional involvement, the artist will generally need to discover the impact ('the dynamic inter-action') of the work on others. Initially it is likely that the work will be shared with an extended audience of one – someone whose judgement is respected and trusted, and someone who will display understanding and appreciation of the artist's intentions and difficulties. In the case of the pupil–artist the 'someone' will most often be the teacher, although the views of (and recognition by) parents and peers are also often sought and valued. The evaluation of a recently completed work is a delicate matter. It is not a neutral commodity that is being discussed, such as a body of factual knowledge or information, but a product which in some strange way might almost be described as organic, so intimately does it represent an extension of its creator.

An effective evaluation will comprise three elements:

a) First, and most important of all, it will *recognise* what has been achieved. Such recognition will include non-verbal as well as verbal response and may also be expressed by sharing the work with a wider audience – for example, through wall display or performance. The essential characteristic of recognition is that it should be totally positive.

b) Second, the evaluation must, of course, contain *constructive comment* which compares the finished work with the original conception. For comments to have constructive value and credibility they need to be based on criteria agreed and readily accepted by both parties involved. In the teacher–pupil relationship this should not be a serious problem since the teacher is likely to be acquainted with the growth process of the work and with the problems encountered by the pupil. The greatest danger is that the pupil's work can become too teacher-conscious, with the young artist becoming more anxious to please than to express. There is then a consequent loss of spontaneity and vitality, and the pupil's work becomes sterile.

c) Third, the evaluation must stimulate sufficient *positive motivation* in the artist to encourage and impel him or her to take the next step along the path of artistic development and personal growth, and thus continue the creative cycle.

Throughout this analysis of the creative process there have been regular references to the availability of resource materials and the need to examine the works of established artists. It makes no sense to separate the language from the literature, creation from appreciation, as has so often happened in the past. Many of us have experience of music 'appreciation' lessons which had much to do with history and dates but little if anything to do with creating music. Recordings of works were played, often accompanied by such instructions as 'Sit up! Listen! Don't talk! It's not funny!'. By contrast, many art lessons focused exclusively on the creative aspect until the upper secondary years. Thus emerged the two cultures of 'school' art and 'real' art! Recently there has been a move towards the introduction of 'critical studies' in an attempt to redress this imbalance.

The process outlined in this chapter equips the pupil with both the tools and the related opportunity to make meaningful contact with works from the 'repertoires' of the various art forms. The emphasis is on the word 'meaningful' since, in an appropriate context, the examination of works will have relevance as well as purpose. The pupil working in a chosen medium – and wrestling with form and other associated technical problems of that medium – will be much more keenly aware of interpretations, responses and technical accomplishments in the works of masters in that art form than he or she would have been as an outsider totally lacking practical experience. The fact is that true awareness only occurs when the situation is relevant: when there is a need to know. On other occasions a feature may be noted but it will be rapidly forgotten. It is a major responsibility of the teacher to ensure that when opportunity or need arises the appropriate material is readily available, thus enabling the pupil to become acquainted with major art works and simultaneously to be made conscious of the tradition to which his or her own creations belong.

The effective expressive arts teacher will be awake to the pupil's changing needs and will know when and how to support, to lead, to cajole, to intervene. He or she will criticise with sensitivity and appreciate with warmth. Perhaps above all he or she will respect the privilege of being allowed to glimpse the young artist's inner world.

CHAPTER 4 THE EXPRESSIVE ARTS AND THE NATIONAL CURRICULUM

The area of experience

Since the publication of their working paper, 'Curriculum 11–16' (the 'Red Book') in 1977, Her Majesty's Inspectors have been advocating a 'curriculum of entitlement' based on originally eight, now nine, 'essential areas of experience'. These are:

- aesthetic and creative;
- human and social;
- linguistic and literary;
- mathematical;
- moral;
- physical;
- scientific;
- spiritual;
- technological.

Whilst the philosophy has not been rejected in the National Curriculum the determination to turn the clock back by retaining subject labels which seem to separate rather than unite disciplines sharing a common area of experience, has caused both dismay and confusion among many expressive arts teachers. Nevertheless, the fact is that art, music, drama and dance all have places within the National Curriculum – art and music as listed foundation subjects, drama within English, and dance within PE. To this extent, the major expressive arts disciplines are all foundation subjects. Fortunately the form of delivery and organisation is left to schools. As it stands, the National Curriculum bears some resemblance to a self-assembly furniture unit for which the plans – the educational philosophy – have been lost. In lieu, the assembler is invited to make of it what he or she will – to give it whatever shape he or she wishes. Inevitably, for some, there will be pieces left over, pieces which will not fit! In the expressive arts the first task is one of devising a strategy for coordinating the disparate elements within a coherent area of experience for *all* pupils.

In 'Curriculum Matters 2: The Curriculum from 5 to 16', Her Majesty's Inspectors offered the following definition of the 'aesthetic and creative' area of experience: *'This area is concerned with the capacity to respond emotionally and intellectually to sensory experience; the awareness of degrees of quality; and the appreciation of beauty and fitness for purpose. It involves the exploration and understanding of feeling and the process of making, composing and inventing'.*

This paragraph is helpful in a number of ways, but in particular it provides a backdrop, a context, for all expressive work in the school. It also reminds us that the expressive arts are not the sole guardians of the aesthetic and creative area of experience. This is an obvious yet important observation to make. Too often, curriculum development is impeded by the shadow of precious subjects in hermetically sealed time-boxes – particularly in the secondary phase. If we are to make sense of an arts curriculum, first we need to understand the contribution of the 'aesthetic and creative area of experience' to the curriculum as a whole, then to determine aims (for the school) within the area of experience. Finally we need to examine structures which enable those aims to be achieved.

In addition to the '5–16' definition there may, of course, be other curriculum statements the school wishes or needs to take into consideration when shaping its own aims. For example, the DES Circulars Nos. 6/81 and 8/83 required each LEA to review its policy for the school curriculum. Both LEAs and individual schools have subsequently produced statements of principles, aims and objectives. Indeed there is a need to update this information in the light of the 1988 Act. Collectively, such definitions, statements, etc., establish the base camp in preparation for the next stage.

Aims

If a school wishes to establish coherence in its provision for the aesthetic and creative area of experience it will be sensible to bring together all who, through their teaching, contribute to this aspect of the curriculum. This group should be charged with the responsibility for producing a set of aims which clearly articulate the school's philosophy and which inform the school's arts policy (see Chapter 8). The aims will provide a spine of reference for all expressive work in the school – wherever it occurs in the curriculum.

Whilst each school will obviously wish to evolve its own set of aims, there are certain broad areas which, no doubt, most will wish to consider. These include:

a) developing in pupils observation, awareness (including self-awareness and the exploration of values) and the ability to make connections with previous experiences;

b) developing imagination, inventiveness, creativity;

c) providing opportunity for the pupil to create, perform and appraise in a variety of media, as appropriate;

d) providing for the acquisition of technical skills, and the opportunity to understand and use structured forms and conventions to express feelings and ideas in a wide range of media; the development of decision-making and problem-solving skills;

e) encouragement of self-evaluation;

f) some reference to the types and range of (sensory) experiences the school wishes to provide;

g) aesthetic awareness, including a critical appreciation of the art forms of other cultures and other historical periods;

h) the provision of an educational environment/ambience conducive to creative expression, i.e. a 'creative' atmosphere providing positive support during the incubation and development of ideas; ample and appropriate stimuli and resource reference materials; the regular use of technical, descriptive and qualitative vocabularies;

i) formative assessment procedures, including appropriate recording and reporting systems; positive recognition of pupils' work, including opportunities for display and performance;

j) stimulation of individual expression and personal growth; equal access for all pupils, and the encouragement of excellence in each pupil according to his or her level of ability.

All expressive work, wherever it occurs, will relate to some of the aims some of the time, whilst the expressive arts will relate to most of the aims most of the time. It is particularly important for expressive arts teachers to give focused emphasis to those aspects which are 'unique' to, or at the very least central to, the arts experience.

Curriculum characteristics
When designing an expressive arts curriculum to achieve these aims it will be helpful to view the problem from the pupil's perspective – to ask what might be considered to be the pupil's curriculum of entitlement *within* the expressive arts area. The four curriculum characteristics used by Her Majesty's Inspectors – balance, breadth, differentiation and relevance – provide a useful framework for this process.

Balance
There should be balance within the arts curriculum. That is to say the pupil should have access to a wide range of art forms including the visual, the verbal and the performing arts. This does not necessarily mean a bit of each discipline all the time, but overall balance over a period of time. A working acquaintance with a wide range of media is particularly important during the primary and early secondary phases. Gradually, as the pupil progresses through the secondary school, personal preferences and aptitudes are likely to emerge and it is right and appropriate that a degree of choice should then be available.

There should also be balance within a particular discipline. We now have a plethora of exciting materials and equipment available in each of the art forms. The arts have entered the age of technology. Perhaps even more significantly, our pupils are children of that age and, outside the school, they are often familiar with sophisticated equipment capable of high-quality performance and a wide range of operations.

The constantly changing scene immediately poses two problems: first, that technological advance is rapidly outpacing the teachers' training and expertise and, second, that with limited financial resourcing, the selection and purchase of expensive equipment is a hazardous business. Neither problem is unanswerable nor, in essence, particularly new. What is new is the scale.

The 'calculators v long division' tension which has exercised the minds of mathematics teachers for several years now, has its parallel in the expressive arts. To turn one's back on modern technology and to insist only on traditional techniques and methods will do little to encourage and motivate the child of the 1990s. Conversely, to overuse, or to abuse, the available technological resources is to debase the arts and reduce them to a 'space wars' type of entertainment activity which has little to do with providing and educating the arts experience. The pupil's entitlement is to a learning programme which balances traditional techniques with opportunities for modern experimental expression: a programme which accommodates the pupil as former, performer, and audience.

Breadth

The expressive arts curriculum should offer breadth in its range of experiences and interests, and should avoid hierarchical, stereotyped divisions. Gradually the hard and fast polarisation between 'high art' and 'pop culture' has dwindled in recent years, and the attitude which says 'this is what I like and it is good for you: that is what you like and it is cheap and nasty', is far less prevalent. But tolerance alone is not enough. Whilst I am categorically not suggesting that the arts specialist should 'sell his or her soul' for pupil popularity, I am certainly of the opinion that arts teachers of today need to be genuinely more catholic in their tastes and understanding than were their predecessors. A disguised, patronising attitude will not do. Sincerity is the first step towards respect, which in turn facilitates both overt and hidden learning experiences. Narrow specialists, however sincere, are likely to have, by comparison, a restricted sphere of influence.

The curriculum should also include some contact with other cultures and other times. Frequently art forms offer the most direct way of getting to grips with the essence of another period or another culture. As a result of the insistent demands of the teacher, a keen geographer can often recite fluently statistics relating to a specific country – such as details of climate and natural vegetation, raw materials, size of population, patterns of agriculture and industry – and yet have no knowledge of how it *feels* to belong to that country. Similarly, multicultural teaching can be long on lists of festivals and religious traditions but short on meaningful experience. The expressive arts can bridge the gap. Art forms regularly use religious symbols, draw upon folk traditions, explore local designs, colours and materials, and evoke national or local atmosphere. From an experiential base questions arise naturally and purposefully, and responses are remembered because they make sense within a broader context. When it is possible to use an artist in residence from the culture being studied, the impact is particularly potent. There is a distinct danger of arts education being too Euro-centred.

Differentiation

Since the expressive arts are concerned primarily with personal response and expression, it is true that differentiation will to some degree depend upon the tapestry of personal experiences of the individual pupil and on his or her awareness, aptitude, motivation and acquired skills. Differentiation may also be considerably influenced by the quality of the stimulus provided by the teacher and by the environment.

Reliance on differentiation by outcome alone is not enough. As stated in 'The Curriculum from 5–16': *A necessary first step in making appropriate provison is the identification of the learning needs of individual pupils by sensitive observation on the part of the teacher'*.

The expressive arts teacher will applaud the suggestion that needs should be identified 'by sensitive observation'. Crude diagnostic tools have little value in this area. Even so, it is certain that particular problems will emerge. For example, there is the challenge to provide opportunity for excellence for each pupil according to his or her level of ability, i.e. both the 'high flier' and the pupil with special educational needs. The range may not be wider in the expressive arts than in other subject areas, but it is often more apparent. Of course, acknowledging a problem is one thing; taking appropriate action to accommodate its solution is invariably more difficult. A first step may well be the acceptance of the fact that the full range of provision required cannot be wholly contained within timetabled class time. Alternative approaches to the use of time will be discussed later.

The curriculum should cater not only for differing ability levels but also for differing personal needs. Pupils do not all require the same prescription. Historically, learning programmes in the arts have tended to be incremental and linear in design – structured, in fact, to meet the needs of the specialist. Since in most disciplines only a minority – in some disciplines, a very small minority – pursue courses through to examination level, a diversification of learning programmes and teaching styles is necessary. A continuous linear programme is neither necessary nor appropriate for many pupils. Differentiation requires flexibility – the flexibility to respond to a variety of needs.

In *The Intelligence of Feeling* (written as a result of his research during the Schools' Council curriculum project 'Arts and the Adolescent'), Robert Witkin says of music teachers observed: *'What was particularly striking was the fact that although they were often very aware of developmental changes that affected the pupils' responses to music, their structuring of the curriculum took virtually no notice of these, nor was there any evidence of a really serious attempt to deal with the difficulties which these changes presented'.*

The criticism here is levelled against music teachers, but experience indicates that other expressive arts teachers are often equally guilty in this respect. It is interesting to note that the choice of literature texts offered to pupils in mid-adolescence in single-sex schools frequently acknowledges the differences between the sexes in matters of taste and preference. Given the opportunity for choice it is unlikely that the boys will be studying *Romeo and Juliet*, *A Midsummer Night's Dream*, or Jane Austen. During the years of puberty, boys feel particularly vulnerable to ridicule and strive to shield their true emotions from others – especially those feelings which may exhibit the more feminine side of their nature. Liam Hudson, the Cambridge psychologist, comments: *'Whether it is through flamboyance, allusiveness, open hostility, academicism, or unconscious all-enveloping restrictions, almost all boys, it seems, set some distance between themselves and the outside world'.*

Yet many arts teachers fail to recognise this characteristic or, to be more accurate, take insufficient positive action to offer boys the necessary protection and security which will enable them to continue their artistic activities without fear of a damaged ego. An adolescent boy will generally work happily through such media as photography, pottery, masks, puppetry or electronic music. In fact, he will accept more or less any medium where his emotions are not exposed directly to a potentially critical audience. To accept this fact has little to do with perpetuating stereotypes but has everything to do with acknowledging reality. We neglect the education of the emotions in the adolescent male at our peril. If, on occasion, positive discrimination/differentiation is necessary, so be it.

Relevance

It will be apparent that the four curriculum characteristics interrelate quite freely and, indeed, many of the aspects outlined above could as appropriately have been included under the

present heading. Three points need stating, or restating, for emphasis:
a) First, relevance involves seeing the world through the pupil's eyes – selecting stimuli relevant to the pupil's experience, yet seeking to increase awareness, helping to broaden vision. For a majority of pupils the parameters imposed by the peer group, TV, the disco, Radio One, are facts of life. The teacher has an obligation to extend these bounds, but to succeed he or she must be honest with him/herself about the point of departure.
b) Second, the curriculum should be directly relevant to the *now*, as well as preparing for the future. An essential feature of the arts curriculum is its capacity to facilitate personal growth through the structured expression of the feeling response. Growth is, by definition, a gradual process. It is within the pupil's entitlement that he or she should be aided and encouraged to savour quality experiences to the full at every stage in his or her development.
c) Third, the expressive arts teacher in the secondary phase should be mindful that through the requirements of the National Curriculum there will be a group of pupils in the upper secondary years pursuing arts courses who previously would have opted out. For these pupils 'more of the same' will not do. A course relevant to their needs is all-important.

Determining content

The key to effective curriculum development rests in the question 'Why?'. Until, at each stage, a satisfactory response to that question has been reached there is little point in progressing to 'How?'. But seldom is the 'Why?' question totally open. It is qualified by circumstances and by who is asking the question. There must be a reason for asking 'Why?' and it is that reason which, to some extent, sets the parameters within which an acceptable answer must fall.

'Why?' can be perceived as threatening, and is frequently uncomfortable. It is a demanding question requiring justification for decisions and choices made and for action taken. In many teaching activities it is easy, with the passing years, to acquire habits and educational clutter – delightfully described in 'The Curriculum from 5–16' as *'content built up by unregulated accumulation or tradition'* – the validity of which may not have been recently scrutinised. If the question 'Why?' is then asked during a review which is likely to result in a curriculum restructuring – such as is required by the introduction of the National Curriculum – it is not difficult to understand the apprehension a teacher may experience.

Conversely, the question 'Why?' can be used constructively to probe and explore alternative approaches to curriculum development, and it is clearly this positive questioning which is appropriate to the present need.

Perhaps the simplest formula for determining curriculum content might look something like this:

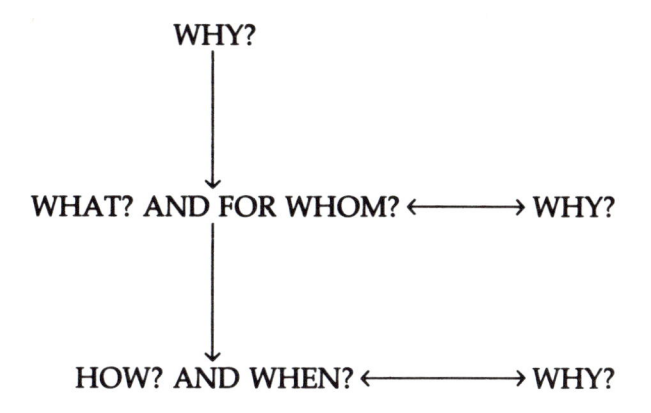

```
        WHY?
          |
          ↓
WHAT? AND FOR WHOM? ←——→ WHY?
          |
          ↓
HOW? AND WHEN? ←——→ WHY?
```

To be completed, of course, this model requires an evaluation stage and a cyclical return to the beginning. But for the moment it is appropriate to consider more closely those stages identified above.

Why?
The initial 'Why?' questions the *raison d'être* for the inclusion of a discipline in the curriculum in the first place. Ample evidence has been given in an earlier chapter to establish the centrality of the expressive arts within a balanced curriculum. By acknowledging the area of experience, and by identifying aims and discussing curriculum characteristics, a spine of reference has been established against which further responses to questioning can be validated and compared. In other words, the parameters within which acceptable answers must fall have been identified.

What? And for whom?——Why?
When developing an expressive arts curriculum for any group of pupils we need to ask, at each stage:

- What skills does the pupil already have?
- What skills do we wish to introduce?

and the important questions:

- Why?
- For what purpose?

Behind these seemingly simple questions lurk the true problems. The first question uses the word 'pupil' in the singular quite deliberately, since the level of skill mastery within a group is likely to vary considerably. The situation is vastly different from a knowledge-based subject where a state of readiness – a required body of learned factual knowledge – can be more precisely identified. In the expressive disciplines there may be a clash between the various needs of the individuals within a group. There may be a tension between the needs of the 'specialist' and those of the 'non-specialist'.

The importance of introducing skills on a 'need to know' basis as a key to the next learning experience has already been stressed. So too has the need to develop appropriate vocabularies to facilitate thinking and expression within the chosen medium. These two aspects must particularly inform the responses to the 'Why?' and 'For what purpose?' questions. But we would be wise to recall what was said about differentiation and relevance, and to ask further:

- Do we wish to introduce the same skills for *all* pupils?

If so:

- To what extent are we requiring 'specialist' skills from the 'non-specialist'?
- What will be the consequences if the 'non-specialist' feels inadequate in the face of such demands?
- What alternative strategies might be adopted to provide the opportunity for each pupil to maximise his or her potential – including the gifted and the less able?

Of course, it is common experience that, particularly during the secondary years, the varying needs become increasingly polarised. Energies should be directed towards exploring and mapping a variety of alternative curriculum routes, and means sought of enabling pupils to transfer between these parallel paths. It can be done – perhaps most effectively through the use of modular approaches.

Whatever strategy and structure is adopted, since skills and content (in the form of subject matter and experience) are so intimately intertwined, it is the choice of content which gives purpose to the acquisition of skills. This is particularly true for the non-specialist – the reluctant artist. Earlier the two essential characteristics of an effective stimulus were identified as:
a) its relevance and meaningfulness to the pupil;
b) its capacity to evoke a feeling response – a response which ultimately finds expression in structured form.
It is the quality of 'arousal' which generates the momentum of the learning process and which, to a large degree, determines the speed with which skills are learned and mastered.

But the definition from 'The Curriculum from 5–16' quoted at the beginning of this chapter is concerned with much more than the acquisition of skills, and in particular refers to the 'exploration and understanding of feeling'. In determining the content of the expressive arts curriculum we therefore need to ask:

- What range of opportunities/stimuli should be provided to encourage 'the exploration and understanding of feeling'?
- Is it possible/is it necessary to produce a development programme to address this aspect of arts teaching?

We might also care to consider:

- Can it be assessed? Should it be assessed? By what criteria would we measure success?

The question of assessment is taken up in a later chapter, but for the moment an illustration will serve to demonstrate the complexity of the task: A short while ago I witnessed a residency by an artist, the impact of which will stay with me for years to come. The artist was a diminutive, quiet young lady. The medium was watercolour. The venue was the grounds of a country house. The time of year was June. The pupils were a mixed bunch of young teenagers from a neighbouring town. They had no previous experience of watercolour. The timetable for the residency meant that the same group of youngsters would return to the house each morning for a week, and a second group would similarly use the afternoons.

As they poured from the bus on the Monday, their arrival was accompanied by all of the yelling, giggling, ribaldry and general giddiness one might expect from a group of teenage 'townies' exposed to the unaccustomed freedom of the countryside. They met the artist, were introduced to the basic techniques and skills, and were dispatched into the grounds to 'work'. Mostly this meant that they congregated in small clusters under trees, chattering noisily until interrupted by the artist who, sitting amongst them, quietly, and seemingly with little effort, produced sketches which won their appreciation and their respect.

As the week unfolded the clusters reduced, and by Wednesday most pupils were working individually, often separated by a considerable distance from their nearest neighbour. Silence and absorption had replaced the earlier chatter, and conversation was, for the most part, reserved for the sharing time at the end of each session.

By the end of the week the quality of work being produced was never less than good and was, in many cases, quite excellent. Aided by the rare June sunshine, the peacefulness of the venue, the quiet disposition of the artist and the non-aggressive nature of the medium, the transformation in the pupils was beyond belief.

Whilst it may not be too difficult to establish criteria which could adequately summarise the quality of the paintings, it is doubtful whether indicators can ever be produced which will satisfactorily reflect the quality of experience enjoyed by those youngsters.

However, returning to the subject of curriculum content, there are teachers who believe that, with the advent of the National Curriculum, *what* is taught will no longer be an issue. This notion that course content will be taken out of the hands of teachers and will be prescribed in National Curriculum programmes of study can be grossly misleading. The DES Circular No. 5/89 makes clear that the *'Orders will determine the minimum requirements for each foundation subject. What is taught may go much wider.'* It also adds *'there will be scope for teaching ... cross-curricular issues'*. In other words, what is taught is likely to remain largely the responsibility of the teacher. All of the evidence currently available supports this view.

How? And when?——Why?

Circular 5/89 also makes clear that *'the Orders will not prescribe teaching methods or approaches'*. Hence the 'How?' question begins and ends with the teacher, who remains a free agent – as long as the appropriate programme of study is integrated into the syllabus and the attainment targets are thereby made accessible. The occurrence of the attainment targets at the ends of the Key Stages will, of course, determine to some degree the phase during which various elements of the programme of study will be included, but serious problems are not anticipated. The requirements of the National Curriculum should promote greater continuity between phases. Certainly the programmes of study will provide a framework of coherence which has not always been apparent in the past. It will be incumbent upon schools to establish effective liaison and communication networks in order that all teachers may know not only *what* is being taught but *how* and *when*.

The 'Why?' question persists as a constant challenge to the teacher to provide a true match between what is being offered and how it is being delivered, with the pupil's needs.

The question of time

Many of the worst fears and apprehensions relating to the introduction of the National Curriculum were stirred by percentage of time allocations mentioned in the original National Curriculum proposals. Whatever the Secretary of State may have intended, and despite his subsequent protestations of being misunderstood, the fact remains that many teachers (including heads) read a great deal into those figures, and in some schools changes were introduced in response to them. A re-carving of the curriculum cake began, with the discovery, of course, that what was needed was a larger cake.

The situation is decidedly clearer now. Again quoting 5/89 we know:

a) that *'the Orders may not prescribe any amount of time which should be spent on any part of a programme of study'*;

b) that *'the Act does not define what is a reasonable time but the intention is that pupils should spend sufficient time in order to undertake worthwhile study in each foundation subject area'*;

c) that *'the Orders may not require particular ways of providing a subject in the school timetable'*;

d) that *'the organisation of the curriculum . . . is the responsiblity of the headteacher'*.

Some teachers have greeted this statement of clarification with relief. Others, with perhaps less faith in their heads and governors, remain anxious. Certainly there are heads who need to be reminded that the National Curriculum is not intended to be the whole curriculum.

The Education Reform Act is bringing about radical change, the full extent of which is only slowly being unfolded. Those who attempt to respond to the new challenges with yesterday's solutions will find life difficult and will be missing the opportunity for creative innovation. The National Curriculum Council's 'A Framework for the Primary Curriculum' signposts likely directions for further development:

a) *'Planning under subject headings does not preclude flexibility of delivery across subject boundaries. It may not always make best sense to deliver all subjects in simple strands in a week'.*
And then:
b) *'As schools become increasingly familiar with the National Curriculum it will become clear that there are many areas where links between the foundation subjects will lead to effective and efficient uses of time'.*

Secondary teachers are advised to pause for a moment to consider the possibilities and implications of these comments, for no longer will integration, interrelationship and overlap be the prerogative of the primary sector. There are many good reasons why, in future, such features are likely to characterise the secondary curriculum also. Some of these reasons may be purely educational. Others may reflect the expeditious use of time and teacher expertise.

It will be helpful to explore more fully a number of different approaches to time:

a) *Protected time/guaranteed time*
This is time set aside when the techniques and skills necessary in a particular art form can be learned, practised and applied. The importance of the acquisition of the vocabulary of a discipline in order to facilitate both thinking and expression has already been stressed. The accumulation of such a vocabulary cannot be left to chance.

b) *The efficient use of time*
Collaboration and cooperation between teachers from different expressive arts disciplines can often lead to the identification of areas of commonality and duplication in, for example, concepts, fields of knowledge and terminology. Sooner or later each of the art forms is likely to refer to form, composition, balance, colour,

rhythm, line, pattern, texture, movement, dynamic, subject, contrast, harmony, discord, counterpoint, shape, tone, register, image, perspective. Yet what do these concepts or terms mean in different contexts? What are the similarities and differences? Is it advantageous to reinforce the pupils' understanding by parallel or shared activity?

It is often a very fruitful introduction to collaboration for two or more teachers from different expressive arts disciplines to select an agreed concept and then for each to work on that concept with the same group of pupils. The benefits are considerable – for teachers as well as pupils! By exploring first the expressive capabilities of the disciplines separately, and then the results of combining art forms, a deeper understanding of the concept is likely to emerge and a 'new' medium is created. Frequently the whole assumes an expressive dimension greater than the sum of the parts. Through television, pop videos, etc., the pupil is familiar with a world in which art forms are constantly combined.

There are, of course, many factors which contribute to the efficient use of time and the effectiveness of the teacher – particularly teacher expertise (and confidence), group size and ability range, and the *quality* of time allocation (i.e. where the lesson appears on the timetable) – but high on any list must also appear clarity of lesson focus and the availability of resources to meet the demands of the task in hand. It is important that the pupil, as well as the teacher, is clear about the focus of each lesson. It is equally important that the appropriate resources are readily available and accessible.

c) *The flexible use of time*

Do all activities benefit from the same pattern of time distribution? What sorts of time patterns are suited to what sorts of needs?

There are basically three main types of pattern: the continuous, the interrupted, and the extended. The 'continuous' pattern refers to the arrangement whereby the pupil receives a regular, weekly time allocation in a particular discipline, uninterrupted throughout the year. For example, in most secondary schools it is common practice for 11 and 12-year-olds to receive two periods of music per week (assuming a forty-period week). By Year 9 the diet may well have been reduced to one period per week.

The important advantage of the continuous pattern is that it facilitates regular contact and therefore assists the incremental accumulation of skills. A possible disadvantage is that 'security of tenure' seems often in practice to encourage an insular and linear approach to programmes of study as well as a disinclination to collaborate freely with other disciplines. Particularly in the lower secondary years such lessons tend to be taught in class or form groups – an organisational feature which, itself, impedes easy collaboration. A further possible disadvantage is that the time available for a single lesson may not be sufficient for meaningful learning to take place. In an attempt to overcome this difficulty some teachers prefer a double lesson per fortnight rather than a single lesson per week.

The 'interrupted' pattern includes the much used, and sometimes abused, carousel or circus approach whereby pupils are exposed to a chosen sequence of disciplines on a rotational basis. A rather more sophisticated version of that pattern exists in the modular curriculum in which the modules comprise self-contained units of study, each with clearly defined aims and objectives. The modules can be placed end to end, or organised in parallel, to build a mosaic of learning experiences and skills.

The advantages of the interrupted pattern are that (a) in the modular form the sharpness of focus tends to encourage 'in-depth' learning, and (b) it provides the opportunity to introduce the pupil to a wide range and variety of experiences in a limited period of time and is therefore useful in 'taster' and foundation courses. The disadvantage is, as the label implies, the difficulty of providing coherence in a course which is by definition fragmented. This problem can be overcome, but it requires careful course construction and supervision, good teacher liaison, and thorough record-keeping which maps the progress of the individual pupil.

The 'extended' pattern refers to the use of occasional 'arts days' or 'arts weeks' or, of course, any other similar block of time. The advantages of promoting an arts week are numerous:

- By abandoning normal time constraints it offers the opportunity to foster experience as well as skills, and allows the pupil to become absorbed in the activity.
- It provides an opportunity to bring together a range of arts disciplines to produce a shared response to a common stimulus, thus acquainting the pupil with the similarities and differences between the art forms.

- It can provide the pupil with access to skills, art forms and experiences not normally available because of staffing and/or timetabling constraints.
- It frequently groups pupils, and also staff, who do not normally work together.

On the negative side, it must be said that the arts week can be used as a ploy by lazy timetablers or uncommitted headteachers to compensate for an inadequate regular time allocation. There is no way in which occasional blocks of time can provide an acceptable substitute for either of the other two patterns, but when used to complement an existing pattern the impact can be considerable. Currently the use of the extended pattern is comparatively limited and it may be helpful to identify some of the key aspects of organisation.

The first two decisions to be made relate to the questions 'Why?' and 'For how long?'. Any teacher or group of teachers contemplating the organisation of an arts week should first determine clearly an appropriate set of aims and objectives. Heading the list must be the aim to provide a positive arts experience for the individual pupil. Such opportunities are rare. It should be a memorable occasion. The purpose behind the week must also be convincing – sufficient to satisfy doubting staff who may be sacrificing 'valuable' teaching time; parents; governors; and 'unenthusiastic' pupils.

The length of the 'week' will depend very much on what it is hoped to achieve and on the scale of the operation. When the project is being organised for a whole year group, for example, evidence generally suggests that the longer the period of time the greater becomes the difficulty of sustaining the involvement of all pupils. Conversely, the shorter the period of time the more directed the project becomes, with a consequent reduction in the opportunity for absorption and experience. Circumstances will dictate the appropriate length.

There are other matters to consider:

- Who will be involved – which pupils? Which staff?
- What is the level of staff commitment? Negativity is damning, particularly when large numbers of pupils are involved. If the commitment is not high in some cases, what alternatives are available? A sub-division of the large group into smaller units,

with each being exposed to a shortened project led by enthusiastic staff? What would be gained/lost?
- What are the optimum requirements in terms of time, pupil numbers, availability of staff expertise, etc., in order to meet the aims and objectives?
- How will the focus/theme be determined? How will it be made relevant to *all* pupils involved?
- How will the initial momentum be generated? (i.e. How can the quality of stimulus be 'guaranteed'?)
- How will it be sustained?
- What course structure will be necessary? What groups? How many? For what duration? (For example, will all activities take the same length of time?) Led by whom?
- How will group membership be determined? Will there be opportunity for choice by pupils? If so, how will that choice be informed?
- What preliminary preparations will be necessary with pupils? For example, will any aspects of the project be prepared in arts lessons during the pre-project period? What will be the 'state of readiness' of the pupils at the beginning of the project?
- What preparation will be necessary with staff? When? Led by whom?
- What steps will need to be taken to acquaint individual staff and pupils thoroughly with their programme and responsibilities throughout the project?
- Is any form of 'sharing' or performance envisaged? If so, what arrangements will be necessary?
- What follow-up will be appropriate after the project?
- Will any form of external expertise be required, e.g. advisory support, members of the community, professional artist(s), etc.? If so, when? For what purpose? Will there be cost implications?
- What materials will be required? Cost?
- What will be the demands on space and accommodation? What will be the impact on the timetable for the rest of the school?
- How will the involvement of individual pupils be monitored?
- How will the project be evaluated overall?

In short, the organisation of an arts week is hard work, but the results can be extremely rewarding and, as one strategy for the delivery of the arts curriculum, the extended pattern should be more widely used.

d) *Overlapping time*
There are disciplines within the curriculum which flatly refuse to be pigeon-holed and constrained by the wishes or whims of administrators and managers. More particularly there are disciplines which emphatically should not be strait-jacketed in that way. In the 1970s, with the emergence of faculty structures and the growth of 'instrumental' learning, art frequently became subsumed in the Craft, Design and Technology cluster and all too often art teachers became 'teachers of design'. Whilst it is important that design should be informed by imaginative and creative thinking it is also important that all pupils should have the taught opportunity to use art – both 2D and 3D – for the free but structured expression of a *feeling* response. To this end art belongs exclusively neither to the expressive arts nor to the design and technology area, but has essential contributions to make to each. The polarisation of fine art and design is unnecessary, unhelpful, and positively impedes the visual education of the pupil.

Similarly, dance occupies the overlap area between the expressive arts and physical education. The expressive without physical technique and coordination is severely restricted and undisciplined. The physical without the expressive is not dance, is not art. Subject labels tell us very little until we know more of the content and how it is being taught. The experience being conveyed is of far greater significance than what it is called!

It is now clear that the attainment targets associated with the National Curriculum programmes of study are intended to be accessible by whatever form of delivery the school cares to use. Thus, a science attainment target may be met through geography, or a mathematics attainment target through science. Similar interchanges are desirable between the expressive arts and related disciplines, and it makes no sense to perpetuate an obsolete cultural apartheid. I shall return to this theme a little later when shaping a timetable model.

e) *The arts across the curriculum*
Mention has already been made of the use of the expressive arts disciplines to illuminate and explore other subject areas. Such techniques as hot-seating, thought-tracking, giving witness and other similar drama conventions, have long since become basic teaching tools of humanities and English teachers, and teachers in the primary phase regularly use the expressive disciplines across all areas of the curriculum. Indeed there is a danger sometimes

that the applied use of the arts can disguise a neglect of skill training in the individual art forms as the pupil moves from topic to topic. In this sense the integrated approach of the primary curriculum is both its strength and its weakness, and it is important for primary teachers consciously to protect a developmental programme in each of the disciplines within the integrated curriculum. The HMI Report 'Primary Education in England', commenting on arts provision, observed that in some schools *'children are working too far within their own capabilities – those in the top of the primary school still doing work of which they were capable much earlier. Sometimes this is because teachers' expectations of them are too low and work lacks direction'.* Often such criticisms are valid where the emphasis is on working *through* the arts rather than working *in* the arts. A balanced curriculum finds opportunity for both.

At the secondary level the relationship and inter-relationship between the subject areas can be illustrated diagramatically:

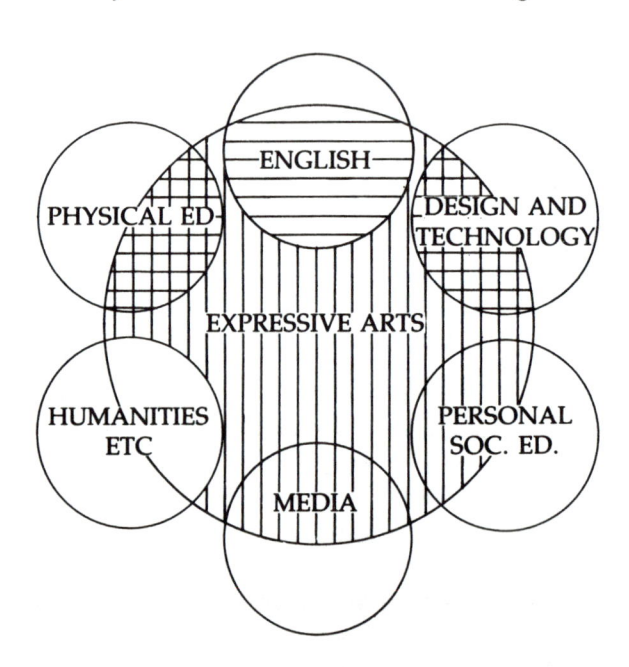

In this diagram the vertically shaded portions relate to areas of study directly covered by expressive arts teaching. Thus that section of the curriculum which is regularly identified as personal and social education is central to much expressive arts work in so far as the arts are concerned, with the structured expression of personal feelings, personal attitudes and personal values. An art form enables an individual to express his or her interpretation or perspective of the world. Often the process of creating and communicating this interpretation will require a closer scrutiny, a keener awareness and a quieter, prolonged, reflective consideration than is characterised by debate or discussion.

Similarly, the creative and interpretative skills essential to media education fall naturally within the expressive arts area of experience, although there are other aspects which relate more naturally to different curriculum or subject areas.

The cross-hatched shading in the physical education and design technology circles refers to the overlap through dance and art respectively, whilst the horizontal shading within English acknowledges that although that subject is normally perceived as being detached from the expressive arts, in practice good English teaching shares many of the same aims, and addresses and provides access to the same area of experience. In his book *English within the Arts*, Peter Abbs comments: 'Nothing would satisfy me more than if ... English teachers formed strong practical alliances with the neglected disciplines of art, drama, dance, music and film and in so doing developed through creative activity the emotional and imaginative energies of our children and adolescents'. There is evidence that such alliances are beginning to form, however slowly.

The humanities circle acknowledges that subject content in the expressive arts is often drawn from other curriculum areas and from the humanities in particular, although the frequency and extent to which this occurs is very variable. Indeed, all these spheres of learning which orbit around the expressive arts are likely to fluctuate in their proximity to the centre.

f) *Extra-curricular time*

Traditionally the arts have offered a range of extra-curricular opportunities to pupils with talent – sometimes outstanding – and/or an appetite for more than can be provided within time-tabled class time. Such activities were often severely curtailed during the prolonged period of industrial action by teachers in the mid-1980s and in some instances they failed to reappear when the troubles had passed. Later, for some schools, the introduction of the 1,265 hours contract for teachers brought its own problems. Nevertheless, most schools are still able to offer a programme of activities to a greater or lesser degree, and it is essential that they should continue to do so for a variety of reasons:

- the talented pupil is able to work with others who are equally, or more, talented and is therefore challenged, stimulated and fulfilled;
- there may be an opportunity to work in skill areas crowded out of, or inappropriate to, the timetabled lessons – for example, choral singing is a much less common class activity than in the past, a fact which gives added importance to the existence of a school choir;
- there is an opportunity to become more deeply involved in the 'repertoire' of the art form, which brings its own demands and its own rewards, as well as providing vital nourishment to the prospective subject specialist;
- freed from the intrusion of the bell, conditions are often more conducive to art-making;
- work undertaken is often prepared for a 'real' audience, thus attaching to the activity credibility and importance.

A school which genuinely aims to provide an opportunity for excellence for each pupil according to his or her level of ability cannot afford to neglect extra-curricular arts provision.

g) *The hidden curriculum*

Whilst the hidden curriculum may not at first appear to be directly related to the use of time, there is little doubt that, as a supportive and enabling factor, it contributes significantly to the effectiveness of the teaching/learning process. There are four factors particularly which facilitate or retard learning:

- The quality of the environment – the ambience, the conditions for learning, the stimulation offered by decor and display, the sense of purposefulness and order without oppression, and so on. There is generally some recognition that art and music require specialist provision, but all too frequently drama and dance are expected to 'manage' in whatever space is available. The fact that even that space may have to be relinquished to accommodate school dinner or external examination arrangements offers a further example of the messages conveyed through the hidden curriculum!
- The accessibility and availability of resources, for reference and for stimulus, as well as material resources for expressive work.

- The attention given to the display and recognition of work produced by pupils. In this context it is important to remember that any material displayed needs breathing space – the larger the breathing space, the greater the impact. At the same time that impact can be eroded through over-exposure. Regular changes of display are time-consuming but essential if a high level of interest is to be sustained.
- Relationships. The special nature of the relationship between teacher and pupil during the creative process has been discussed. Of course, such a relationship can only be fostered not forced, but once established it clearly maximises what can be achieved during any fixed period of time.

The timetable

The discussion thus far has provided a framework for an arts curriculum. For many the challenge lies in moving from theory and philosophy to timetabling in practice. To demonstrate that this can be done, a timetable model, suitable for the first two years in the secondary phase (now Years 7 and 8), has been added as an appendix to this chapter. It has been placed there because it is inevitably technical in certain aspects and because such detailed working is in no way essential to an understanding of the rest of the chapter. Nevertheless, the model addresses important concepts – particularly relating to overlap – and readers generally may well wish to explore these ideas. The model does not seek to answer all problems but it does provide a structure through which solutions become accessible and opportunities are offered (as, for example, combined arts or cross-curricular projects). There is an assumption that the timetabled diet will be supplemented and enriched periodically by arts 'weeks', artist residencies and opportunities for experiential learning.

Organisation

The faculty and departmental organisations found in most secondary schools can inhibit the flexible and overlapping arrangements advocated in this chapter. This is particularly so where heads of faculties or heads of departments are 'territory' conscious, or where headteachers feel that it is necessary – perhaps for administrative reasons – to group subjects into academic cooperatives. All too frequently faculties or departments become introspective and often resist contact with other curriculum areas.

However strong the dislike for 'vogue' labels, the titles of 'coordinator' or 'team leader' both imply concepts more in sympathy with the ideas expressed here. Thus the coordinator would be responsible for coordinating and mapping all expressive arts work and experience, wherever it occurred in the curriculum, and for ensuring that it related to the stated aims and objectives and by so doing formed part of a coherent pattern. The coordinator would ensure compatibility and coherence between the syllabuses, assessment, recording and reporting procedures of the various expressive arts disciplines and would have overall responsibility for arranging collaborative projects.

'Team leader' is a term associated most naturally with sport, where increasingly the practice is to use a squad of players from which an appropriate team will be selected for a particular match. Similarly a school will generally have more 'players' with their various individual talents than are used for any specific 'timetable match'. The challenge is to select the best team for the task.

This system enables a teacher to drift temporarily into or out of a squad and, indeed, to participate as a member of more than one team. The team may also wish to borrow expertise from further afield – from other curriculum areas, or from the community. For example, it is not uncommon to find a talented photographer lurking behind a most unlikely subject label! Or, a mathematics teacher may at some stage have followed a training course in dance and may be better suited to the teaching of dance than the physical education specialist. Wherever the talent lies it should be used. To continue the sporting analogy, a bank clerk may be an outstanding opening batsman for the local cricket team at weekends. But there is no conflict of interests. On Saturday he will be answerable to the cricket captain: on Monday to the bank manager. So with the curriculum model discussed above, the dance teacher does not have to belong exclusively to either the physical education team or the expressive arts team but can, and should, at various times be a member of each. Like the bank clerk, the dance teacher will then be answerable to more than one 'captain'.

The model implies that there can be two types of team leader: one, with responsibility for a team teaching a discrete discipline, and a second type with responsibility for leading a team promoting a specific collaborative programme. In practice it is likely that for the first type the responsibilities will be permanent, e.g. the team leader for drama will almost certainly have responsibility for the development of the subject throughout the school, and that responsibility will be ongoing. By comparison, the second type of team leader can be appointed for a specific short-term or one-off project. For example, it may be that the school wishes to organise an arts week. The responsibility for organising and planning the week could be delegated to a team leader who would lead and coordinate the activities of a team of teachers drawn together for that purpose. The appointment would be temporary. An attractive feature of this delegation strategy is that comparatively junior staff can be recognised and encouraged and can be groomed for permanent responsibility.

Administratively, curriculum funding would be channelled through the coordinator, with 'capitation' allocations devolved for discrete disciplines and for special projects according to their various needs. In the primary school it is equally important that the responsibilities associated with these two roles should be clearly defined and allocated. The point has already been made that within the integrated approach there is a danger that developmental programmes can be diluted, lost or forgotten. The appointment of a teacher as coordinator or curriculum leader can do much to avert this potential problem – at the same time giving both cohesion and coherence to the arts programme, as well as identifying areas for in-service training for teachers.

To summarise

This chapter has been concerned with providing a framework for the reappraisal of the expressive arts provision in a school and has mapped a possible route for improvement and/or change. That route began from a philosophical base – the identifying of the essential areas of experience, the call for a clear set of aims and objectives, an exploration of curriculum characteristics – and insisted that all curriculum development should constantly be required to satisfy the question 'Why?'. From the philosophical it turned to the practical. It encouraged an awareness of the differing characteristics of alternative time patterns and suggested that the delivery of the arts curriculum need not be restricted to one pattern only. In particular (in the appendix) it offered a curriculum and timetable model for a foundation course in the secondary phase which facilitated both the teaching of discrete discipline skills and also provided opportunity for interrelated or combined arts work – a model which could be adapted to accommodate a variety of patterns. Finally it referred to possible styles of organisation which could effectively coordinate and implement the range of activities discussed.

The introduction of the National Curriculum is demanding the most rigorous rethink about the purpose and organisation of schooling since the introduction of state education. School curriculum reviews are being superseded by development plans. If these plans are to be relevant and meaningful to the 1990s they must be scrutinised from a 1990s' perspective. The thinking must avoid being intellectually crippled by the concepts and jargon of a past era. It is a time for new questions to be asked, since old questions are likely to produce old responses and old frustrations. Fresh thinking and fresh demands are likely to point the way to a need for radical change. The agenda identified in this chapter seeks to promote that process. Viewed in this light the requirements of the National Curriculum can be seen as an exciting challenge rather than as an ominous threat.

Appendix
A timetable model for years 7 and 8

The value of the time available can be greatly enhanced by the style of organisation adopted – that is, by placing disciplines into structures and time-patterns which promote coherence, and which both overtly and covertly facilitate intrinsic relationships. Since some expressive disciplines have natural links in more than one direction, it makes sense to dissolve arbitrary boundaries wherever possible and, conversely, to reinforce natural grouping.

When discussing 'overlapping time' above, reference was made to art and dance as links between the expressive arts and related disciplines. This overlap can be illustrated diagramatically:

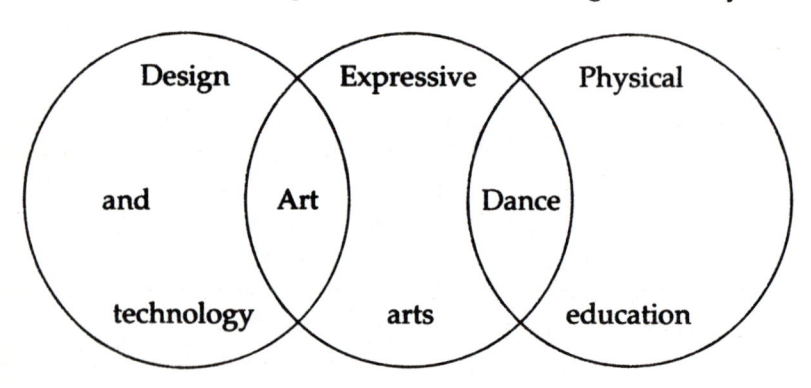

Design and technology / Art / Expressive arts / Dance / Physical education

The model which follows demonstrates one way in which theory can be translated into practice. For the purposes of this exercise a number of conditions have been assumed:
a) The timetable is designed for pupils in the first two years of the secondary phase. A major aim of such a timetable must be to provide a broad foundation – an exposure to a wide range of disciplines – enabling the pupil to make an informed choice of preferred disciplines at a later stage. To reflect the Key Stage divisions which are characteristic features of the National Curriculum there is a case for extending the foundation course to include the first *three* years of the secondary phase, but many schools believe that some initial options choice should be possible in Year 9. This facilitates the positive rejection of a discipline with which the pupil has no affinity (for example, it may be counter-productive to insist that *all* boys continue with dance – although I would vehemently defend their right to have the choice) and allows more time for the sustained study of a discipline to be developed further in Years 10 and 11. Such choice must, of course, be qualified by the requirements of the National Curriculum, and may be influenced by localised systems of education. In some LEAs a three-tier system involves transfer between schools at the beginning of Year 9 and it is seldom helpful for any choice to be made solely on the basis of experience gained in another establishment.
b) The chosen cohort comprises approximately 108 pupils – the equivalent of a school with a 4 Form Entry (4 FE). There are two reasons for this choice:

- because of staffing constraints, the problems in the small school are often greater than in the larger schools, i.e. there are fewer alternatives available;
- schools with 6 FE or more tend, in any case, to split the year group into smaller units.

c) An analysis of a random group of schools indicated that the average aggregate amount of curriculum time allocated to the areas of design and technology, physical education and the expressive arts was 30% – or twelve periods in a forty-period week.

Inserting this information into the DES formula for calculating curriculum provision, we find that we are entitled to 48 periods of basic provision. To this we can add a bonus (again averaged from the same group of schools) of 37.5%, the equivalent of 18 teacher periods, giving a total availability of 66 teacher periods. So, for each of the 12 periods we shall have available 5 teaching groups, with some teaching periods spare to use as we will – perhaps, as the worked model suggests, by dividing two PE groups between 3 teachers to accommodate dance.

d) It was decided to offer the following disciplines:
Physical Education (i), Physical Education (ii), Music, Drama, Art (i), Art (ii), Home Economics, Technology (i) and Technology (ii). Physical Education (i) indicates the 'games' end of the continuum with Physical Education (ii) suggesting the gymnastics/dance aspect. Art (i) and (ii) can perhaps best be thought of as very loosely representing 'fine art' and 'design-based' approaches respectively, with both providing access to a range of activities, media and experiences which refuse to be categorised.

Similarly Technology (i) and (ii) indicates that there will be a range of styles and activities, perhaps including control technology and craft realisation of design briefs. The actual choice of disciplines in any particular school will obviously depend upon local circumstances, both in terms of staff expertise and working spaces and resources available.

e) Because of time and staffing constraints it is not possible to continue all of the disciplines all of the time. It has therefore been decided in this model to divide the school year into four × ten weeks time blocks with a changed timetable pattern in each block. Nevertheless, it is possible to offer varying degrees of continuity in the generic areas of physical education, performance arts, visual arts and technology. It is also worth re-stating the assumption made earlier in the chapter, that the regular timetabled provision will be supplemented and enriched periodically by arts 'weeks', artist residencies, and opportunities for experiential learning.

Reading the Curriculum Costing Model

The 108 pupils have been divided into five groups identified as A, B, C, D and E.

Figures refer to the number of periods allocated to each group against a particular discipline. The total for each horizontal line must be twelve – assuming a forty-period week (i.e. twelve = 30% of the taught timetable). Groups have been combined for physical education purposes, e.g. groups A and B are timetabled together, as are C, D and E.

The figures linked by lines denote some form of alternating or rotational arrangement. For example, in the PE (ii) provision

CURRICULUM COSTING MODEL

		PE (i)	PE (ii)	PE (Dan)	Music	Drama	Art (i)	Art (ii)	HE	Te (i)	Te (ii)
10 WEEKS	A	2 }	2 — 2 } 3 t'chs		2	2		2		2	
	B	2 }	2 — 2 }		2	2		2			2
	C	2 }	2 — 2 } 3 t'chs		2	2		2			2
	D	2 }	2 — 2 }		2 — 2	2			2	2	
	E	2 }	2 — 2 }		2 — 2	2			2	2	
10 WEEKS	A	2 }	2 — 2 } 3 t'chs		2 — 2	2			2	2	
	B	2 }	2 — 2 }		2 — 2	2		2	2		2
	C	2 }	2 — 2 } 3 t'chs		2	2		2			2
	D	2 }	2 — 2 }		2	2	2			2	
	E	2 }	2 — 2 }		2	2		2		2	
10 WEEKS	A	2 }	2 — 2 } 3 t'chs		2	2	2			2	
	B	2 }	2 — 2 }		2	2		2		2	
	C	2 }	2 — 2 } 3 t'chs		2 — 2	2	2		2	2	
	D	2 }	2 — 2 }		2 — 2	2			2	2	2
	E	2 }	2 — 2 }		2 — 2	2			2	2	2
10 WEEKS	A	2 }	2 — 2 } 3 t'chs		2 — 2	2		2	2		2
	B	2 }	2 — 2 }		2 — 2	2	2		2	2	
	C	2 }	2 — 2 } 3 t'chs		2 — 2	2	2		2	2	
	D	2 }	2 — 2 }		2	2			2		2
	E	2 }	2 — 2 }		2	2			2	2	
Block 1		10	5(6)	5(6)	8	8	4	6	4	6	4
2		10	5(6)	5(6)	8	8	4	6	4	6	4
3		10	5(6)	5(6)	7	7	4	6	6	6	4
4		10	5(6)	5(6)	7	7	4	6	6	6	4
Total t'cher per'ds		40	20(24)	20(24)	30	30	16	24	20	24	16

(The totals in brackets indicate the number of teacher periods required to accommodate a three-way split of Groups A and B for dance.)
The total number of teacher periods used in any one week = 60(62), i.e. within the 66 periods allowed in the brief.

it is suggested that the groups rotate on a system whereby one group is taking dance while the other two groups are taking physical education, e.g.:

	Week 1 Periods		Week 2 Periods		Week 3 Periods		Week 4 Periods		Week 5 Periods	
	1	2	1	2	1	2	1	2	1	2
Group C	D	PE	PE	D	PE	PE	D	PE	PE	D
Group D	PE	D	PE	PE	D	PE	PE	D	PE	PE
Group E	PE	PE	D	PE	PE	D	PE	PE	D	PE

and so on.

Effectively this means that each pupil receives a dance lesson two weeks in every three, and receives a minimum three periods of physical education every week. A similar pattern is indicated for Groups A and B by dividing the total number of pupils in the two groups into three subgroups, but this may not be necessary or desirable. It is obviously possible to use a dance teacher and a physical education teacher, with the groups receiving one period of dance each week, i.e.:

	Week 1 Periods 1 2	Week 2 Periods 1 2	Week 3 Periods 1 2
Group A	D PE	D PE	D PE
Group B	PE D	PE D	PE D

and so on.

Where the circled music and drama figures are linked by a line, the implication is that during that block music and drama will alternate – i.e. two periods of music one week, two periods of drama the next week. Or, of course, one of each every week, but with a consequent reduction in the amount of time available in which to achieve meaningful lesson development. (In this respect the needs of music and drama tend to differ from those of dance, where a 'little and often' is generally the preferred pattern.) A degree of economy is introduced in the music and drama areas because (a) in music, the demands of the National Curriculum require an increased amount of music in the upper secondary years and this time has to be saved from somewhere (unless additional teachers are found!) and (b) there is often a shortage of drama expertise in schools. If schools are able to offer more, good!

A pupil in Group A will therefore follow a curriculum which comprises:

FIRST TEN WEEKS BLOCK:

Two periods of PE (i), one of PE (ii), one of dance, two of music, two of drama, two of 'design', and two of technology

SECOND TEN WEEKS BLOCK:

The arrangements for PE and dance continue, two periods of music and drama alternate on a fortnightly basis, two periods of art (from the 'fine art' end of the continuum), two periods of home economics, and two periods of technology

THIRD TEN WEEKS BLOCK:
The arrangements for PE and dance continue, music and drama each receive two periods per week, the 'fine art' and the technology continue
FOURTH TEN WEEKS BLOCK:
The arrangements for PE, dance, music and drama are as for the second block, two periods of 'design', two periods of home economics, and two periods of the alternative style of technology

(Because the model uses an odd number of teaching groups, practical timetabling constraints dictate that not all groups will receive exactly the same provision in any one year. However, over a two-year period such anomalies can be redressed).

The totals reflect the balance provided between the different areas. Thus there are sixty periods of PE, sixty periods of performing arts (music and drama), and sixty periods of home economics and technology. Twenty periods of dance and forty periods of art provide the 'overlaps' and blur unnecessary dividing lines.

The timetable realised

The illustrations below demonstrate translations of the costings model into practical timetable terms for the first two time blocks.

TIMETABLE: FIRST TWO BLOCKS

		1	2	3	4	5	6
BLOCK ONE	A	Mus	PE(ii)/Da	Dr	Art(ii)	PE(i)	Te(i)
	B	Dr	PE(ii)/Da	Art(ii)	Mus	PE(i)	Te(ii)
	C	PE(ii)/Da	Art(ii)	Mus	Dr	Te(ii)	PE(i)
	D	PE(ii)/Da	Mus/Dr	Art(i)	Te(i)	HE	PE(i)
	E	PE(ii)/Da	Dr/Mus	HE	Art(i)	Te(i)	PE(i)
BLOCK TWO	A	Mus/Dr	PE(ii)/Da	HE	Art(i)	PE(i)	Te(i)
	B	Dr/Mus	PE(ii)/Da	Art(ii)	HE	PE(i)	Te(ii)
	C	PE(ii)/Da	Art(ii)	Mus	Dr	Te(ii)	PE(i)
	D	PE(ii)/Da	Dr	Art(i)	Mus	Te(i)	PE(i)
	E	PE(ii)/Da	Mus	Dr	Te(i)	Art(ii)	PE(i)

There are, of course, numerous alternative solutions possible, some of which may be determined or constrained by such factors as the number of suitable spaces available for physical activities.

The figures 1 to 6 across the top indicate *double* periods, totalling the twelve periods per week required to deliver the proposed curriculum. Since there are only five school days in the week it will be necessary for at least two of these double periods to fall on the same day. Indeed it could well be advantageous to place two doubles next to each other, thus producing a half-day block of time and simultaneously facilitating a wide range of interdisciplinary or combined activities. For example, the possibilities offered by placing blocks 2 and 3 together are considerable. Such a framework would provide a sound basic framework within which to explore various approaches discussed earlier in this chapter.

For teachers inexperienced in timetabling who perhaps may wish to adopt the model, one further point needs to be made. In order to provide each group of pupils with four periods of home economics teaching, twenty teacher periods will be required. Since the timetable is constructed in double periods it is not possible to divide the twenty periods equally between the four timeblocks. Therefore two of the timeblocks will have two double periods and two will have three double periods – making ten double periods in all (i.e. twenty periods). For practical timetabling purposes it is generally quite difficult, if not impossible, to change a teaching pattern half-way through the year. The teacher will therefore need to be available for three double periods throughout the year, even though only two doubles will be required in two of the blocks.

Once a solid foundation in the expressive arts has been established during the primary and early secondary years, the pupil will be equipped to exercise a degree of choice as he or she progresses into Key Stage 4. Whatever the range of courses offered, the responsibility of all charged with designing and implementing the arts curriculum must be to ensure that the curriculum characteristics identified above are satisfied. This is particularly necessary for pupils who may be pursuing courses which do not lead to external examination. The demands of the National Curriculum must be accessible through time patterns which promote opportunity for *meaningful experience* as well as for the acquisition of skills.

CHAPTER 5 ASSESSMENT AND EVALUATION

The debate regarding assessment in the arts is no longer concerned with *whether* the arts should be assessed, but with *how* they should be assessed. Best reflects contemporary opinion when he states: *'There can be no educational justification or accountability for an activity for which no coherent account can be given of the answerability to reason of assessment and progress'*.

The demands for assessment are numerous, they are clear and they can be justified. First, there is a public demand – the public in this case comprising parents, employers, school governors, the LEA, elected representatives at both local and national level, and other 'providers'. Their requirement is the demonstration of what pupils know and what they can do. It is about identifying standards which can be analysed and compared, as well as providing school leavers with certificates and, hopefully, with enhanced prospects of employment. Regrettably, in many instances assessment becomes the instrument which produces the statistics with which to compete – with neighbouring schools, with neighbouring Authorities, with past standards. In this context assessment has to do with 'being better than' – if only to enable Mrs Brown to prove that Billy Brown is better than Jimmy Smith, or that School A is better than School B. The latter point, of course, takes on a new significance with the introduction of devolved funding to schools. It is an identified aim of the Local Management of Schools to create competition between schools, to respond to market forces as a means of raising 'educational' standards in schools. Since the level of funding received by a school will be heavily dependent upon the number of pupils on the roll, the incentive will be great and the reward could be substantial.

Second, teachers have a need to assess. Indeed, they need assessment for a variety of reasons. Without some form of assessment it is not possible to assist the progress of the individual pupil. Conversely, assessment can be a significant catalyst for change in the pupil's progress and level of achievement. Again quoting from Best: *'To fail to assess is to fail to teach properly. What form that assessment should take is, of course, another matter'*.

Without assessment, how can the teacher steer and chart pupil progress? Closely associated with this fact is the whole concept of continuity, not only of the individual but also of groups of pupils, both within schools and between phases in education. Without assessment there is no point of reference. What is more, the point or points of reference must be identifiable and clearly understood by all the parties involved. Secondary and primary school teachers must be speaking the same language – but we shall return to this theme later.

Then, too, the teacher needs assessment to test the success or otherwise of teaching strategies. The teacher is, after all, an essential partner in the learning process who needs some assessment of the effectiveness of his or her contribution.

Third, the pupil needs assessment. It is his or her right! For all of us, whatever our position or status, there is a desire to know whether we are performing to the satisfaction of others whose judgement we respect and value, or whose support we need. The nature and purpose of the assessment may well change with the passing of time, sometimes being used to motivate or, at other times, to diagnose a weakness. Ultimately, at the age of 16, it is likely that the pupil will seek some form of external assessment and recognition of his or her achievements. The pupil's prospects of success will be greatly enhanced if, during the preceding years, his or her progress has been sensitively monitored and assessed, and his or her educational needs have been responded to imaginatively and purposefully. It is a major responsibility of schools, and of individual teachers, to devise processes and teaching styles which facilitate such success. Schemes of work may provide the map, but the pupil also needs a 'you are here' arrow and compass.

The demands for assessment, then, are considerable and will not be denied, and in this respect the arts are not excepted. Traditionally, assessment has been a very controversial issue among arts teachers, and the tension between subjective judgement and objective criteria has regularly and frequently been hotly debated. For many, the form of assessment which results in awarding to a piece of art work a single grade or a percentage mark is a betrayal of the special relationship between teacher and pupil outlined in an earlier chapter. Indeed, much of the hostility towards assessment in the expressive arts has grown out of years of 'enforced' acceptance of assessment procedures totally alien to the creative process. In part, it was the price paid for seeking recognition and parity with other subjects in the curriculum.

I recall only too well that, as a young music teacher in a grammar school in the early 1960s, I was required at the end of each term to award to each pupil in the lower school a percentage mark plus a grade. I was given a 'curve of distribution sheet' indicating how many As, Bs, Cs etc, could be allocated, and an accompanying instruction indicating the fixed percentages I had to use for the top and bottom pupils. Once this had been achieved, the marks were then scaled down to ensure that when the totals were aggregated for all subjects, music would receive its proper weighting, i.e. it was less than half as important as the academic subjects!

I am not for one moment suggesting that such attitudes and formulae still persist, but it is certainly true that in many schools arts teachers are expected to conform to assessment policies and to adopt assessment techniques which are totally unsuited to expressive arts teaching. Against this backcloth it is small wonder that arts teachers anticipated the recommendations of the Task Group on Assessment and Testing (TGAT) with foreboding and deep suspicion, and when the initial proposals for a National Curriculum were announced there was considerable relief that the expressive arts seemed to be escaping the imposition of programmes of study and attainment targets. That was in 1987.

Two years later, at a conference on 'The Future of the Arts in Schools' held at the University of Warwick, some 90% of the 500 delegates, drawn from all quarters of the arts education world, voted in favour of attainment targets for the expressive arts. What was interesting about the vote was that it was not particularly the result of a debate in the hall but was rather the spontaneous response to a casual question from the chairman, Professor John Tomlinson. So positive and so immediate was the reaction to the chairman's invitation to vote that many of the delegates were clearly startled to find themselves suddenly part of such a large majority, and it was apparent that their surprise was shared by the collection of eminent educationalists on the platform.

Changing perceptions of assessment

So why has there been this apparent *volte face*? Why are arts educators now prepared to recognise the need for, and positively encourage, the development of programmes of study and attainment targets? I would suggest that there are five main reasons, each in its own way significant:

a) Initially there was confusion over terminology. For some time the term 'assessment' was seen by many as being synonymous with 'quantification', and since there are experiences within the creative process which essentially cannot be measured, the credibility of any system which could employ crude instruments of measurement, especially when associated with some externally imposed 'test' or 'task', was questioned. It is difficult to appreciate now just how strong was the link between educational measurement and accountability in 1987. The obsession with quantification led no less a figure than Baroness Warnock to advocate graded tests for the arts – a series of summative benchmarks which would motivate pupils and raise standards. The graded examination structure of the Associated Board of the Royal Schools of Music was cited as a possible model. Within the prevailing climate arts teachers feared that a national assessment scheme might well reflect such thinking and that schools could be left with a straitjacketed, examination-led curriculum – a curriculum which lurched from one milestone to the next with no opportunity for the traveller to enjoy the scenery.

Gradually the wider interpretation of the term 'assessment' has become clear, the extensive range of assessment styles has been demonstrated, and the threat of narrow, progressive, summative goals has been removed. The language is more clearly understood. Dialogue is possible.

b) There has been time for a closer scrutiny of the TGAT report and there are aspects, central to that report, which the arts teacher finds reassuring. For example, paragraph 4 directly responds to a fear voiced above: *'The assessment process itself should not determine what is to be taught and learned. It should be the servant, not the master of the curriculum. Yet it should not simply be a bolt-on addition at the end. Rather, it should be* an integral part of the educational process, *continually providing both "feedback" and "feedforward"'*.

The emphasis is mine. For the arts teacher, process is particularly important – often more important than the product. The product represents but one phase in the process – albeit a crucially important one – and there are occasions, particularly in drama, when to focus excessively on the product may well distort the balance of the educational process as a totality. Whilst paragraph 4 is clearly referring to whole curriculum issues, it is nevertheless identifying two principles important to each of the individual disciplines which comprise the component elements of the curriculum.

The arts teacher will also be more than pleased to endorse paragraph 221: *'For the system to be formative it must produce a full and well-articulated picture of the individual child's current strengths and future needs. No simple label 1–6 will achieve this function, nor is any entirely external testing system capable of producing the necessary richness of information without placing an insuperable load of formal assessment on the child. The formative aspect calls for profile reporting and the exercising of the professional judgement of teachers'.*

Again features which find resonance in good arts teaching are emphasised. Because of the nature of most arts activity, formative assessment, however informal, provides the essential substance of which the dialogue between teacher and pupil is made, and in this context the arts teacher could applaud also paragraph 28: *'We see confidentiality as crucial if assessment is to serve a positive role. . . . We recommend that all assessment information about an individual be treated as confidential and thus confined to those who need to know in order to help that pupil'.*

Only slowly has the impact of the TGAT report been appreciated by many arts teachers. Only gradually have they awakened to the potential for positive and welcome change contained within the report's recommendations.

c) An important contributory factor to the 'change of heart' has been the publication of material relating to the National Curriculum core subjects. These publications have removed the lingering fears associated with the possibly prescriptive nature of attainment targets. In moving from one era of development to another there is always a problem that new terminology will not be immediately understood, whilst the terminology which *is* understood will bring with it a legacy of past interpretations and connotations. Such has been the case with attainment targets. Until they could be clearly illustrated in the context of the new programmes of study it was not possible to dispel unnecessary fears or misconceptions. The reality has proved to be much less forbidding than the horrible imaginings. It is reassuring to see the TGAT recommendations finding acceptance.

Arts teachers have also come to appreciate the opportunity for coherence provided by programmes of study and the accompanying attainment targets. It is an understatement to suggest that arts programmes in the past have not been characterised by a degree of coherence. Indeed arts teachers have often been portrayed as isolationists, mostly unaware of what is happening in any other arts area and totally oblivious to the main stream of education in the school, let alone to the happenings in feeder schools or other establishments. But the Education Reform Act is reaching those parts no other Act has reached and many teachers are now seeing positive benefits from the introduction of the National Curriculum, of which coherence is one.

d) Teachers are now prepared to explore the idea of assessment components and objective criteria. It is sometimes necessary to remind ourselves exactly how rapidly arts education has developed in recent years. The Gulbenkian Report was published in 1982, and the Assessment of Performance Unit's discussion document on 'The Assessment of Aesthetic Development' followed in 1983. Both publications, in their separate ways, were ahead of their time and served to plot the path for those who followed after. The vote at Warwick University demonstrated that the pack is now closing up on the original pacemakers and a wary eye is being kept on the new front-runners, The National Curriculum Council (NCC) and the School Examination and Assessment Council (SEAC). The APU's 'framework for assessment' at the very least offered a 'framework for discussion' and is likely to provide a useful starting point for the NCC arts working parties. A significant fact is that there is a willingness among arts teachers to work together on this – a willingness to seek out common components and attainment targets which can be shared by all of the expressive arts disciplines.

e) The final reason is quite simply one of status. Among the National Curriculum subjects there is perceived to be an identifiable hierarchy, indicated by those subjects which enjoy core status, and then defined by the pecking order of the remaining subjects within the four-year agenda. In this context, teachers are tending to the view that if the arts subjects are not accorded full status, they will be devalued and may face an uphill struggle in the battle for staff, time and resources.

The individual delegates at Warwick University may have been influenced by any one, or all, of the above reasons. The staggering fact remains that the decisions were individual decisions, unorchestrated, and yet so many had arrived at the same conclusion.

Two significant factors

Having declared a readiness, almost an eagerness, to proceed, arts teachers will nevertheless be anxious to ensure that any proposed framework for assessment is wholly appropriate to the expressive arts and is not merely the transposition of a formula generated to meet the needs of other curriculum areas in changed clothes. The expressive arts provide a *different* way of knowing and it is important that the factors which contribute to that difference should be recognised during both the assessing and reporting processes. To make this point is not to plead a special case for the arts, it is merely to state the obvious. To move from one curriculum area to another without acknowledging the changed needs is as futile as travelling from one country to another without changing currency.

I would suggest that two factors in particular assume a greater significance in expressive arts assessment than in the assessment of other disciplines. They are:

- the impact of assessment on the individual;
- the importance of process in arts education.

Both aspects have already aroused some comment and discussion above and in an earlier chapter, but it will be helpful to elaborate on these thoughts a little further.

There is abundant evidence to support the observation that pupils are more vulnerable to criticism when involved in artistic expression than in any other curriculum activity. Somehow the criticism cuts more deeply and the injury lasts longer. (It is interesting that the image of 'injury' should have sprung so naturally to mind!) Ask any randomly selected group of five adults about their artistic abilities and three will claim that they have none. If pressed, they will often draw upon the opinions of arts teachers, perhaps expressed many years previously, opinions which discouraged them from taking any further active interest in the arts. Why is there this reaction? The point has been made that the expressive disciplines demand a higher level of personal involvement, a greater investment of self, than many other areas of learning and consequently the ego is on trial. The theory is easily tested. The reader has only to think back to his or her own schooldays. It may sometimes be difficult to recall *what* we were taught in the arts but it is not difficult to recall *how* we were taught. We remember people as people, not necessarily as teachers. Those who found time to understand us, and who acknowledged and patiently nurtured our fumbling efforts, we respected and responded to. Their influence was positive, regardless of our level of ability in their discipline. In any activity in which the personal feelings of the pupil are deeply involved or exposed, sensitivity and respect are essential qualities demanded of the teacher. Because of the unique nature of each art form, if the pupil is turned away from that discipline through a feeling of inadequacy he or she will be denied access to a whole area of experience unreachable by any other means. At least in curriculum areas dominated by 'bodies of knowledge' other routes remain open. In the arts, careless criticism regularly causes permanent withdrawal.

Comparison, too, can be a powerful demotivator. Of course assessment is not possible without comparison. Assessment without comparison is reduced to description, and description alone has very limited value. But it is not comparison *per se* which creates problems. It is the nature of the criteria chosen which determines the level of enthusiasm with wich comparison is welcomed. For example, there is no problem if the pupil's own previous work is used as the benchmark, or if the criteria are externally selected or imposed. Difficulties begin to arise when comparisons are made between peers, particularly when the pupils belong to the same teaching group. Discussing differences of approach or interpretation can be very positive, but suggesting that one is better than the other can be counter-productive. The arts are not about competition.

The human condition, which is so vulnerable to criticism, is equally available to praise and positive comment. Exactly what motivates a pupil depends to some extent on the educational climate in which the pupil is working. In a school which is dominated by grades and percentages and where the competitive spirit is prized, then clearly most pupils will strive to respond to the expectation of the regime. But such an ethos is in conflict with the natural course of events following the completion of a piece of art work, which tends to be:

a) Stage 1: Personal assessment. (In this act the pupil is in good company. Throughout the story of the Creation in Genesis we read at the end of each phase that God looked upon what he had created 'and it was good'!)
b) Stage 2: Recognition – approval by peers;
– approval by teacher;
– approval by parents.
Perhaps the overriding need of the artist, young and old alike, is to have his or her work recognised and valued. The importance of 'recognition' should not be underestimated. Often the opportunity to display work or to share a creative experience with others is a particularly potent motivating force, and if the teacher's prime purpose is to improve the quality of the pupil's work then the energy released through the recognition of work is a characteristic to be appreciated and used. It is more important to the pupil to have his or her work valued than to have it measured.
c) Stage 3: Reward – evidence of progress;
– allocation of marks/grades.
At this stage, comparison with past performances enters the frame and the pupil seeks reassurance that progress is being made.

The significance of marks/grades depends, as suggested earlier, on the ethos of the school. In sympathetic environments it is not until the later stages of the secondary phase, and the dawning of external examination demands, that importance is attached to regular grading.
d) Stage 4: Status – ultimately status is achieved through success in an external examination, usually the GCSE.

(It is interesting to reflect that these four stages of motivation have direct parallels for most of us in our daily lives. We do our jobs to the best of our ability, but we like our efforts to be recognised by others. After a while we anticipate that the quality of our work will be tangibly rewarded, and that ultimately we shall be accorded the status we feel we have earned.)

The second factor referred to was the importance of process in arts education. Again, even within the expressive arts camp, there are shades of opinion. Eisner writes: *'Simply knowing the final score of the game after it is over is not very useful. What we need is a vivid rendering of how that game is being played'*. Whilst Best comments: *'The creative process cannot intelligibly be regarded as logically distinct from the creative product. That is, the process can be identified only by the product; the process can be described only by reference to the product. So to assess and consider creativity we have to concentrate on the* product.'

If we are considering the full range of activities within the expressive arts area of the curriculum then the two views are not incompatible. Let us take three examples which illustrate the point:

a) a solo instrumental performance in music. Best would be right: it would be possible to deduce from the performance a great deal of information regarding the process which led to the final performance. The preparation in technical skills, the level of musicality and interpretive skills, and the understanding of the context would be apparent in the performance. It would be possible to provide an assessment of the pupil's level of achievement *if* the performance programme contained sufficient variety of style and was typical of the performer's usual standard.

b) a musical composition or piece of art work. If the assessment is to be formative and of maximum value to the pupil, the assessor will need evidence of work undertaken during the process, such as preliminary sketches, drafts and re-drafts. An assessment based on product alone will not be enough. During the process alternatives will have been considered, choices and decisions will have been made. It is important for the assessor to know *what* alternatives have been considered and *why* particular decisions have been made. Whilst we might agree with Best that *'the process can be described only by reference to the product'*, we begin to acknowledge Eisner's view that knowing only the final score is not very useful.

c) creative work in dance and drama. Much dance and drama work is process-orientated rather than product-orientated – particularly so in drama. As a consequence we are often concerned in these two art forms with expression which is essentially ephemeral and fleeting in character. To disturb the balance, because it happens to be easier to assess product than process, would be contrary to the concept of curriculum-led assessment and would raise serious doubts about the validity and credibility of the assessment itself.

At the same time it has to be acknowledged that assessing the ephemeral poses problems for which I am not sure we yet have the answers. There is, for example, the problem of securing and retaining evidence for verification and moderation purposes.

Whilst the use of video cameras can help, the videoed recordings of dance often tell us more about the camera operator than about the dancers! Then, too, there is a need for highly developed observational skills – knowing what to look for, as it may only happen once. The APU document called for 'trained observers', whilst Eisner advocates the 'educational connoisseur': *'Educational connoisseurship is the art of appreciation. It is the art of having developed a highly differentiated array of anticipatory schemata that enable one to discern qualities and relationships that others, less well differentiated, are less likely to see'*. The fact is that much work remains to be done in this area and teachers must be given training opportunities to develop and share appropriate skills.

An assessment profile

So what are the profile elements (attainment targets?) which offer the basis for a shared assessment policy across the expressive arts? I would suggest there are four:

- response to a stimulus;
- knowledge;
- skills;
- appraisal.

These are consistent with the 'creative process' outlined earlier, and the last three elements in particular share much common ground with the APU model.

The *response to a stimulus* is a crucial stage in the arts experience and yet it is extremely difficult to assess. The position is well summarised by Hudson's comment, albeit in a different context: *'A tension exists within any research discipline between what the research worker can measure and what he would like to measure'*. The arts assessor knows the problem only too well! The response phase is one during which connections are made with past experiences. Only a small percentage of these connections will be shaped in conscious thought, and even fewer will be articulated in any form of 'product statement'. The response to the stimulus gives birth to the process. Helping pupils to identify their own feeling responses and training them to make connections with previous experiences is an essential part of arts teaching. It is important that the pupil's development in this area should be recognised and commented upon. But making contact with the pupil's inner processes is difficult. Dialogue, of course, is important but is often inadequate. Eisner suggests possible approaches: *'How does one make sense of what is non-observable? One way is to make inferences from observables to what is not observable. Manifest behaviour is treated primarily as a cue, a springboard to get someplace else. The other way is to "indwell", to empathise; that is, to imaginatively participate in the experience of another. The difference between the two is subtle but important. In the former, observables are used in a kind of statistical fashion; one intuitively (or statistically) estimates the probability that this behaviour means one particular thing or another. There is no need for empathy. The latter banks on the observer's ability to imaginatively project himself into the life of another in order to know what that person is experiencing'.*

Whether or not one wholly shares Eisner's view it is certainly the case that effective assessment of this dimension can be made only by someone who has known the pupil well over a period of time. It is then possible to pass objective comment on such matters as changed levels of sensitivity, awareness, range of response and interpretation. In a summative context where the assessment is made externally (e.g. by an assessor or examiner who has little or no direct personal knowledge of the pupil), 'response to a stimulus' will carry different connotations which may be more profitably and more appropriately subsumed within the other elements.

The *knowledge* component will need to address the pupil's development in three particular areas:

a) awareness of the unique nature of the medium and understanding of its particular qualities;

b) knowledge of conventions, techniques and forms of expression appropriate to the medium;

c) acquisition of technical, descriptive and qualitative vocabularies to facilitate communication.

Collectively these three aspects provide a framework within which development can occur and can be assessed. Good teaching will anchor them into a historical and cultural context which will enable the pupil to relate his or her own art work to an evolving tradition. By so doing, 'knowledge about' is converted into 'understanding'.

The *skills* involved in the creation of an art piece in any medium can again be divided into three categories:

a) those skills associated with the generation, researching and development of ideas;

b) skills concerned with formal structure and organisation;
c) language, communication and presentational skills.
Every piece of creative art work will draw upon each of these three skills categories, although there may well be a change of emphasis from one assignment to another. Despite the close interrelationship it is important to the pupil's development that each of the skills areas should attract separate comment and assessment.

For the majority of pupils *appraisal* is likely to be the most enduring artistic activity, and yet it is the one which has traditionally received least recognition. Appraisal is important in two forms: in the pupil's evaluation of his or her own work, and in his or her evaluation of the work of others. In either case appraisal and evaluation can only meaningfully take place against an identified set of criteria. Self-evaluation will be achieved by comparing what has been produced with the initial intentions, and by assessing the effectiveness of the numerous decisions and choices made during the creative process. The appraisal of the work of others will require criteria such as those identified in the knowledge and skills sections above. Then the pupil with knowledge of an art work's context (i.e. its cultural and historical genre), an understanding of the medium and its expressive forms and conventions, and experience in the appropriate skills and vocabulary, will be equipped with the tools to make an informed judgement – however inadequate or incomplete that judgement may be in the early stages. The APU document emphasises:
'Education in the arts should consist largely in eradicating unsupported idiosyncratic responses, and in encouraging a progressively enlightened attention to objective features of the works considered and created'.

But there is an additional dimension in the appraisal of an art work. Heyfron writes: *'The subjective in art, unlike in science, is fundamental to an understanding of artistic phenomena. It is not a fringe factor. The notion of quality in music, literature or painting would be unintelligible without reference to a work's capacity, or lack of it, to move, absorb, transfix, entrance, excite, and captivate its audience. These "subjective" states are not reducible to "objective" features of a work. They deserve equal consideration. The former states may be rendered intelligible with reference to the latter, but that should not minimise their significance'.*

This is a crucially important point, for the pupil must never be given the impression that appraisal of an art work is concerned only with the intellect and not with feeling. It is the use of each to support the other which we must seek to cultivate. The need for balance between the two is well expressed in the APU document: *'It is of the first importance that artistic appraisal should be personal, in the sense that children should experience and think about the work for themselves. Yet it should also be objective in the sense of being appropriate to discernible properties of the work, and in the sense that children should develop the ability to give sound reasons for their judgements'.*

The reference to personal response raises the issue of personal preference. Most young children and many adolescents are quite catholic in their tastes. It is a function of the teacher to equip the pupil with the tools and criteria which will help the pupil to develop his or her own critical faculty. It is *not* the function of a teacher to make comparisons which establish in the pupil a feeling of guilt because he or she enjoys an 'inferior' art work or art form. To attack or defend a piece (whatever the art form) purely on the grounds of its supposed generic status is to demonstrate a lack of artistic integrity and to display a degree of prejudice incompatible with good teaching practice. As the pupil acquires and exercises the tools of appraisal, so his or her tastes too will modify. But the ability to appreciate a work is not necessarily the same as liking the work. We have already established that it is quite possible to admire the aesthetic qualities and the mastery of technique and style in a work without actually liking it.

The appraisal element in the profile is concerned with the pupil's ability to express and substantiate his or her opinions – to offer 'sound reasons'. There is ample scope to encourage personal response and to accommodate personal preference.

The completed profile will provide a comprehensive assessment of the pupil's progress in a particular art form. Naturally the balance between the weightings of the various elements will fluctuate, both between individual assignments and at various stages in the pupil's development. But a need to comment regularly on progress in each area will ensure that no aspect is neglected. Of course, the essential partner in the assessment process is the pupil who needs to know what counts as achievement. Within each of the elements at any given time the criteria must therefore be clearly understood and owned by the pupil.

Record-keeping and reporting

For the educational process to be effective there must be coherence between the work completed, the style of assessment and the methods of record-keeping and reporting. Discord between any two of these components may well undermine the whole process. Set against the backdrop of the programme of study in any discipline, the record-keeping system will need to fulfil two functions:
a) to log the work done;
b) to record the pupil's progress and level of achievement.

The record is, of course, much more than an *aide memoire* for the teacher. It provides information which will help to identify the pupil's future needs, and which will form the basis for reports to parents and governors, or, on occasion, to the teachers of another school. Referring to the National Curriculum reporting ages, the TGAT report makes an interesting observation: *'The choice of the reporting ages ... carries with it the implications that the teachers responsible for making the assessments will not be those responsible for acting upon them. ... This feed forward role is diminished if the assessment of a pupil's progress in a subject is designed to produce only a single overall score'*.

The latter point has been adequately covered already, but the issue of progression warrants further comment. The problems associated with progression in a discrete discipline within the particular phase may well need revisiting, but they are generally far less acute and more easily managed than those relating to progression between phases, e.g. from primary to secondary. If secondary teachers are to build on information received from the primary schools then it is essential that there is sufficient detail available, and that teachers from both phases are 'speaking the same language'. This can best be achieved by teachers from a cluster of schools, secondary and primary, meeting together (preferably on a regular, even if infrequent, basis) to exchange and share perceptions and opinions. At the very least there should emerge a common system of assessment and reporting, or sufficient understanding to make differing systems compatible. It is not enough to know that in the year before the pupils transferred, their learning in the expressive arts took place through a series of cross-curricular topics including pollution and Victorian England. The secondary teacher needs to know in addition what specific skills were taught: he or she needs to have some idea of the new starting point for each pupil.

There is, of course, an assumption being made that the secondary school's own house is in order and that the various expressive arts disciplines are all using an agreed assessment framework, preferably along the lines of the profile outlined above. Certainly a shared policy is important for reasons of coherence mentioned above, and to facilitate clarity of communication, both at the giving and receiving ends. An agreed framework also makes possible a collated overview of a pupil's development in the arts generally – a task seldom undertaken and even less frequently commented upon.

Finally, on this theme of recording and reporting, I would plead for the profile approach to be sustained through to the reporting to parents stage, and for the 'single overall score' to be firmly resisted. I would also urge that comments relating to the pupil's attitude towards the discipline should be marginalised unless they are significant. Often such comments convey more about the teacher than they do about the pupil, and the parent is no doubt already well acquainted with the pupil's feeling towards the subject! The purpose of any report is to provide information in as much detail as possible within the constraints of the chosen system. For the expressive arts the profile offers an admirable system for indicating clearly what the pupil *can do*.

Evaluation (of teacher performance and the learning experience)

Pupil achievement is inextricably interwoven with teacher performance, and it is likely that both will be constant targets for evaluation at a variety of levels. Self-evaluation is reflex behaviour to most teachers, who in turn expect their work to be monitored within the school as well as by inspectors from outside. For evaluation to serve any useful purpose it needs to address two issues: effectiveness and efficiency. It would be fair to suggest that, by inclination, most classroom teachers are rather more interested in effectiveness than in efficiency, whilst those with managerial or inspectorial responsibilities would wish to view the two more equally.

Effectiveness has been defined as

$$\frac{\text{achievement}}{\text{objectives}}$$

which is helpful as long as there is agreement about what constitutes achievement. Perhaps one definition might be that effective teaching enables the pupil to advance his or her level of learning, understanding or performance. Certainly the quality of work produced by the pupil, compared with his or her own previous standards, must be a significant indicator. But the teacher will also wish to explore the effectiveness of varying teaching styles, the inspirational qualities of different stimuli, and the success or failure of strategies devised to motivate the recalcitrant or the unsure. To be effective is a priceless reward in teaching, and whilst effectiveness may be made manifest through a pleasing or satisfying art piece produced by a pupil, it can just as readily be conveyed through a brief glimpse of the pupil's increased awareness, a fleeting facial expression or a twinkle of excitement in habitually dull eyes.

A parallel equation for efficiency states that

$$\text{efficiency} = \frac{\text{output}}{\text{input}}$$

For evaluators, not the least attractive feature of this equation is that many of the associated factors can be quantified. It is not difficult to calculate how much is spent on capitation, material and human resources. Equipment can be seen, accommodation can be measured, staffing ratios can be monitored and the presence of a resident artist is usually self-evident. The output indicators may be more contentious. Heads, governors and parents could be looking to external examination results as one measure, with perhaps the number of pupils opting to continue their studies beyond the age of 14 in a particular discipline as another. The number of pupils receiving tuition on orchestral instruments is a familiar yardstick, whilst, for some, the public image of the school as transmitted through the expressive arts will be significant.

The relative merits of such indicators can be argued at length and with passion. Certainly expressive arts teachers will be quick to point to the ease with which sound educational philosophy can be usurped by the application of some of the indicators identified above. The central aim of arts education – to provide *every* pupil with skills and experiences which facilitate access to another way of knowing – has little to do with the quality of external examination results or even the public image of the school.

A style of evaluation (like an assessment process), whether related to an individual teacher, a 'faculty' or a school, should be the servant and not the master of practice. It should be capable of responding sensitively to ideological and qualitative aims as well as to accountability indicators. The purpose of an evaluation is invariably to monitor existing standards and to identify areas for improvement. But within that general remit it is essential for specific criteria to be agreed and owned by the party being evaluated, if the evaluation itself is to enjoy credibility. These criteria will assist the design of the evaluating profile framework, which clearly will change from one evaluation to another depending on the particular focus of the individual evaluation.

Used creatively, evaluation can be the teacher's greatest ally, providing recognition and confirmation of what has been achieved and perhaps offering support to requests for additional resources or training. Reference was made earlier to the pupil's right to assessment. The teacher similarly is entitled to have his or her work evaluated, and it is with this positive attitude of *entitlement* that evaluation should be viewed.

CHAPTER 6 PROVIDING THE TEACHERS

'What kind of teachers for what kind of curriculum?'

The question is borrowed from Malcolm Ross's *Arts and the Adolescent*. There it is asked more specifically of dance education, but it is such a fundamental question that it is certainly pertinent to the present discussion. It would be interesting to know how often individual headteachers have pondered this problem in relation to the expressive arts and how many have shied away – no doubt postponing a response until the matter becomes more urgent! For most it is not a comfortable question. The vision to know what you want in this sense is, in itself, a creative process. Sadly there are those whose vision is blurred – who see through a glass *very* darkly!

It has been suggested that there are two distinct types of curriculum model: the 'assembly' model and the 'design' model. The first comprises the drawing together of separate pockets of learning, rather in the manner of a DIY piece of furniture – but occasionally with additional pieces bolted on, such as externally generated initiatives. The second is tailor-made. It implies a purposeful control and shaping of events – the moulding of component elements and constraints (physical, human and legislative) into an imaginative and coherent whole. It has both the flexibility and creative energy within it to accommodate and integrate externally generated initiatives. Too often the 'assembly' model has about it a pragmatic 'victim of the circumstances' inevitability. At worst it is characterised by a reactive, almost fundamentalist response to the letter of the law, since such an approach offers security and a safe haven. Thus there are schools doggedly attempting to hang on to the misleading and misguided subject divisions and time allocations outlined in the original National Curriculum proposals. In the expressive arts, some schools have failed to replace or appoint drama or dance teachers because those disciplines are not separately identified in the list of National Curriculum foundation subjects. Others, in a mistaken flash of enlightenment, have gathered together those subjects which they choose to define as 'the arts', have put a head of department in charge and assumed that all has been resolved!

The sense of vision referred to in the opening paragraph needs to encompass three strands: (a) a clear philosophy of what the area of experience is about, and the entitlement of each pupil in relation to the area of experience; (b) the organisational structure necessary to translate the philosophy into a practical reality; and (c) the nature and quality of the ambience required to support this development. Earlier chapters have been much concerned with addressing these issues and should have offered some guidance to the headteacher reflecting on 'What kind of teachers for what kind of curriculum?' as well as suggesting possible shapes the 'design' model curriculum might explore.

Once a clear picture has emerged of what the school wishes to provide, the second obvious step is an analysis of the existing scene, for it is the mismatch between the two which will determine the programme of needs.

The changing scene

It is also an interesting exercise to compare the findings with those which would have been produced from a similar review analysis just three or four years ago. Even the most cursory of comparisons will serve to emphasise the speed of change in education.

Consider, for example, the use of technology in expressive arts work. Developments in the application of computer technology to design, and similarly to music composition, have made the computer a basic tool of the trade. Four years ago such activity was confined to a handful of enthusiasts scattered throughout the length and breadth of the country who believed that the new technology had something to offer, even though the software available at the time was gimmicky and tiresome rather than innovative and excitingly creative. Since then a marriage has taken place between the software designers and the clients or, in many instances, the teachers themselves have learned something of the designer's skills. They have become more aware of the capabilities and the most effective ways of using the new tool. Not only have these developments increased the range of expressive capabilities in the respective art forms, they have also made sophisticated expression accessible to pupils of modest ability who lack the required advanced skills at a personal level and for whom, as a consequence, such experience would previously have been unattainable. In the past, the feeling of inadequacy could well have turned these pupils away from the arts experience – probably for life. Now the facility to create a respectable design or composition encourages the pupil to go on, to explore further. With the barrier overcome, new horizons often beckon. In any secondary school an art or music area without at least one computer would today belong to an under-resourced minority, such has been the scale of the technological explosion.

The recent past has also seen the introduction of the General Certificate of Secondary Education. In all disciplines there has been a 'shake-up' of syllabus content, sometimes resulting in a change of emphasis, sometimes in the introduction of new areas of study. There has been an accompanying move towards the increased importance of experiential learning, and coursework has become a significant component in final assessments. Thus the teacher has been required to address three particular areas of change:

a) *New content*
Dependent upon the vintage and training of the teacher, this may make considerable demands. In the expressive arts this is likely to amount to much more than merely the assimilation of an additional body of knowledge, and the development of new or dormant practical skills requires a gestation period which will not be rushed. In music, for example, the ability to teach improvisation skills is not easily acquired by teachers whose training may have been academic rather than practical in character.

b) *New syllabus structure*
Not only have courses for the examination years had to be restructured but, in many instances, the influence has been pervasive, and courses for the lower secondary years have been adjusted and amended to facilitate coherence and progression.

c) *Assessment techniques*
New areas of study and the increased emphasis on coursework have necessitated changed assessment techniques. A major challenge has been, and still is, the collecting and retention of evidence sufficient to confirm and verify assessments made by teachers in the classroom. In the visual arts there is no problem, for exhibition and display are an integral part of the creative process. But for the performing arts, where the process is often by

nature ephemeral, there can be considerable difficulties. Recording, whether audio or video, requires the acquisition of additional skills. The quality of recording can be crucial to the final assessment, and demands specialist (i.e. experience and understanding of what to look for in that art form and in that context), technical and creative competence. Lack of competence not only results in an inferior product but also in a waste of that very precious commodity – time. Indeed, in some circumstances, there is a very real danger of pupils spending more time on recording than on being taught.

The point is also worth making that the collecting of evidence is common to all curriculum areas. Humanities, language and science teachers wish to record field-trips, visits, interviews, experiments and research, and assumptions are often made that professional competence and expertise relating to photography, sound and film rests with the expressive arts teachers. Such a belief may or may not be justified. As a generalised expectation it can at best be described as rash.

In addition to GCSE requirements, assessment, accountability and profiling are all issues which have been brought (quite rightly) under closer scrutiny. Records of Achievement feature prominently and the expressive arts teacher invariably has important contributions to make. Thus, whilst most of the changes outlined are commendable and to be welcomed, the fact remains that for many teachers, although their job descriptions may not have changed, what they are actually doing now is appreciably different from what they were doing four years ago.

The new circumstances and revised needs may not have been easy to accept for some teachers. Changes which necessitate the acquisition of new skills, almost by definition declare other skills to be inappropriate or redundant, and these latter are likely to rest with the more mature and experienced teachers. In some instances the situation may have been exacerbated where, perhaps as a result of falling rolls or amalgamation, teachers find themselves confronted with a different clientele and equipped with skills which no longer match the task.

This description of some of the recent changes affecting teachers in general – but for our purposes, expressive arts teachers in particular – serves to highlight a number of issues:

a) First, there is no reason to believe that the speed of change is likely to decrease in the near future. On the contrary, the 'bedding-in' of the Education Reform Act and the National Curriculum will generate constant change for a considerable period to come. In these early days the preoccupation is with the implications of programmes of study, attainment targets and the problems associated with resourcing following the introduction of the Local Management of Schools. But it is certain that attention will soon be turned to styles of learning, the restructuring of subject areas, and so on. In short, the first requirement of a teacher of the future will be flexibility and the capacity to absorb, and flow with, change.

b) Second, we are reminded of the built-in obsolescence of initial teacher training. It is true that many courses currently on offer, particularly in the expressive arts, are plainly inadequate. Others are good. What we have to acknowledge is that even the best courses have a 'sell by' date and it is the responsibility of all in education – the DES and the LEA, as well as the school itself – to ensure that in-service structures exist to recharge and revitalise as the need arises.

c) Third, it is already apparent with the advent of LMS that governors and headteachers have acquired a new sensitivity to the cost of teachers as a resource, and in particular to those teachers who are earning the largest salaries. It is essential that if the arts are to sustain a high position in the priorities stakes when funding is apportioned, every opportunity must be taken to demonstrate that the school is getting value for money through the quality and relevance of the courses available to all pupils. Arts teachers must generate imaginative in-service programmes which enable all teachers to keep abreast of latest developments – programmes which increase the currency value of expressive arts staff.

Among these developments must be included the process of 'departmental' restructuring, the need for which has been accelerated by the introduction of the National Curriculum and the extension of TVEI. In a rapidly growing number of schools, expressive arts teachers are being drawn together either formally or informally and the days of isolationism are passing. However welcome the change may be educationally, for some the shift of emphasis represents a considerable culture shock. Seemingly in no time at all, horizons have broadened from the four walls of the classroom to those of the expressive arts area, and then beyond the school to the cluster group of neighbouring schools as the issue of continuity of learning between phases, as well as within phases, assumes a new importance. Relationships have changed or are changing. New links are, of necessity, being forged. Teachers who in the past may have looked to in-service training as the opportunity for personal professional development are discovering that the balance has tilted in favour of programmes which respond first to the needs of the school, the department and/or other diverse groups, and only second to the needs of the individual. With the delegation of in-service funding to schools, this change of emphasis is hardly surprising.

Generic categories of training needs

What is emerging from this discussion is the fact that, over and above initial training, there are certain generic categories of training need which must be addressed if schools generally are to get the teachers they require. The effectiveness of those teachers will depend upon the quality of the compensatory, creative and support training offered locally.

First there must be training programmes which clarify beyond reasonable doubt what is expected of the individual teacher. In recent years the introduction of the teachers' contract (1,265 hours) and the prevailing climate of accountability have conspired to make detailed job descriptions the norm rather than the exception. But changing curriculum requirements have comparatively little to do with job descriptions. They can, however, create a nervous uncertainty among teachers until the actual requirements of programmes of study and attainment targets are known and understood. Much damage has been done as a result of misinformation and speculation. There is an added advantage that well-planned training programmes explore as well as inform and, as a consequence, encourage more imaginative and varied responses and interpretations from the participants.

Second there is a constant need for training in new skills which may complement, replace or update existing skills. Examples have already been given where the need for such training has been initiated by the introduction of the GCSE. In that instance training programmes were focused on content, learning styles and assessment techniques. It is certain that the introduction of the National Curriculum will make similar demands.

But the National Curriculum will make other demands too,

particularly through the inclusion of music as a foundation subject up to the age of 16 years. Currently the music provision in most secondary schools comprises regular lessons in Year 1 and 2 (often two periods per week in a forty-period timetable), rather more patchy coverage in the Year 3, and a reduction to examination sets only in Years 4 and 5. Teacher appointments have obviously been made with this style of timetable commitment in mind. In keeping with the historical tradition outlined earlier, until fairly recently the music teacher has often been academically trained and has been expected to focus on examination work, music in the lower school and extra-curricular activities. This is a far cry from the full ability range teaching which will now be required in the upper school. Not all music teachers have either the inclination or the expertise to provide for non-specialists in this age range and it is possible, indeed probable, that some will seek other paths to glory! It is absolutely crucial that adequate training programmes are provided as a matter of urgency to meet this identified curriculum demand.

In the case of primary teachers the demand is not so much created by changing circumstances as by inadequate initial training. An HMI survey, 'Quality in Schools: the Initial Training of Teachers', carried out between 1983 and 1985, found *'inadequate provision for the expressive arts in virtually all the institutions'*. In 1986 the National Foundation for Educational Research published its report, 'The Arts in the Initial Training of Primary Teachers'. The NFER survey confirmed the HMI report. Without quoting at length the evidence provided it is worth noting two extracts:

a) *'The findings from this survey confirm that teachers specializing in the upper primary age ranges are likely to receive a somewhat limited training in the arts. The lack of compulsory B.Ed and PGCE courses in music, drama, and particularly in dance/movement for these teachers could have serious effects on the breadth of the arts curriculum for children in the upper primary and middle school. It could also reflect on the status of these art forms if they are seen as something children 'grow out of' at around the age of seven or eight'.*

b) *'Teachers frequently expressed the view that they lacked the confidence and expertise to provide adequate arts experience for their pupils'.*

It seems reasonable to assume that the training before the period under survey was not markedly superior to that between 1983–6 and that, even allowing for a possible revolutionary improvement post-1986 (of which there is no evidence), an overwhelmingly high percentage of our primary teachers will have been inadequately prepared for expressive arts teaching. Following the NFER report, the Gulbenkian Foundation, in conjunction with the NFER, convened a seminar of HMIs, LEA advisers, teachers and teacher educators to share views on what was needed to improve the situation. A report of that seminar, 'The Arts and the Primary School: Reforming Teacher Education' written by Malcolm Ross, sets out a number of recommendations. It is too early to assess the impact of this succession of documents. In the meantime we are left with the not inconsiderable task of retrieving the situation through in-service structures and other strategies. Much good work has been, and is being, accomplished by individual LEAs, as the evidence from the 'Arts in Schools' Project demonstrated, but the provision remains patchy and the problem is ongoing.

Small schools also generate a demand for training in new skills. In the past, the term 'small school' has referred particularly to rural schools – the small village schools with a handful of teachers or less. But there is a sense in which the plight of the rural schools may not be so great as that of some larger schools. First, the rural schools have been with us for many years. Second, they are so numerous that they command attention. And third, most LEAs with large rural areas to serve have devised strategies to compensate for any lack of specialist provision. My concern here is for those schools which fall into an educational poverty trap. They are too large to attract additional support and perhaps have been unable to replace a specialist teacher because of a falling-roll situation. The choice is either that specialism can no longer be taught or that it may be taught by a teacher less qualified – a teacher in need of training. This particular scenario may be even more prevalent in the secondary than in the primary phase, and the consequences on occasions can become dire. For example, if the departing specialist is the school's sole dance or drama teacher a substantial number of pupils will be deprived of access to an important area of experience. It is unlikely that in-service training alone can compensate for such a loss but it at least represents a positive response – as an alternative to wrath, despair and a host of other unproductive protestations – and offers the pupil some opportunity for continued study in the discipline, however limited that opportunity may be.

The third generic area relates to training for managers – and I am suggesting that there are separate training needs for senior and middle management tiers. The opening of this chapter demanded of headteachers, and others in high places, a sense of vision. Now, it is a common feature of vision that if you are not facing in the right direction you will fail to see what you are looking for! If you are facing in the right direction, and particularly if you are in the company of an expert, you may see a very great deal more than you anticipated. There must be training opportunities for headteachers and other members of senior management teams which not only indicate the general direction in which to look, but which also illuminate the significant individual characteristics of the scene. This latter aspect of the training might well be approached by involving the participants in creative workshop situations. In the changing educational climate it may also be helpful to include governors in similar training programmes. The written word (whether from the National Curriculum Council or the LEA) needs to be supplemented by opportunities for dialogue and interaction. Argument is less potent than experience. The first task is to tempt senior managers, governors *et al*, by whatever means are deemed necessary, at least to turn in the right direction.

At the middle management level there is an urgent demand for training programmes geared to the needs of the new style of expressive arts head of department, coordinator, team leader, or whatever the local terminology may be. A glance through the advertisements of past copies of the *Times Educational Supplement* will indicate the extent to which collaborative structures have proliferated. In many instances schemes are at the stage of conception rather than in their infancy, and schools are looking for leadership and direction. Such has been the speed of development that demand has outpaced experience. There is no shortage of teachers who firmly believe in a multi-discipline or combined arts approach. Many of these teachers undoubtedly have the personal qualities essential to leadership, but at this time their elevation to a post of responsibility would be made on the basis of potential rather than extensive experience. There is no doubt that in this area training provision is currently trailing behind demand. Many of the issues raised in this book – the establishing of aims and objectives, the creative process, the use of time, styles of assessment, training programmes, and so on – should be considered essential elements in such a training course.

The fourth generic area also relates to training needs brought about by change. References have been made to 'new awarenesses', which we may describe as horizontal and vertical. Horizontal awarenesses are those which familiarise teachers with the skills, knowledge and processes in other disciplines and in other curriculum areas. Vertical awarenesses are those concerned with continuity in the learning experience. A combination of the two is essential if coherence is to be achieved. It follows, or should follow, that the development of these awarenesses cannot be left to chance. It is also the case that since so many teachers are reaching a similar point in their own learning experience at the same time, there must be an opportunity to share, to discuss and to explore, and there must be provision of a training framework which indicates possible directions and offers support for growth. Without such a framework there is a distinct possibility that the positive challenges offered by change will be replaced by the negative forces of bewilderment, frustration and cynicism.

The fifth generic category returns us, full cycle, to the needs and aspirations of the individual teacher. If the educational environment is fertile it will encourage self-evaluation and stimulate the desire to improve, and must in turn offer the opportunity for that improvement to be achieved. Teaching skills either grow or they fossilise. There is little distance between the two, and the transition from one condition to the other is not necessarily apparent to the teacher involved. In the preface to *Art Education: Heritage and Prospect*, Anthony Dyson writes: *'Just as the painter steps back from his canvas the better to apprehend the composition in its entirety, soon returning to intimate tactile contact with its surface, so the teacher of art needs constantly to adjust his focus'*. He adds: *'Louis Arnaud Reid's argument is that it is important for* all *arts teachers to distance themselves from their subject in this way – to attain that capacity for detachment that leads to conceptual understanding'*.

Although it is dangerous to generalise, it may also be true that the amount of time spent in 'detachment' needs to be proportionate to the amount of time spent at the 'surface'. Certainly the range and variety of support available needs to be considerable. It also follows that the initiative for 'detachment time' may not always come from the teacher. With the introduction of appraisal systems and the delegation of financial control to individual schools, it will be interesting to monitor the various strategies adopted for obtaining value for money from the teaching force.

The careful and discriminating use of in-service training offers one alternative but, in the circumstances described, its application requires sensitive awareness both in diagnosis and placement.

The analysis of needs: the development plan

These five generic categories provide a useful framework for the analysis of training needs and professional development both generally and, in our case, when applied to a specific curriculum area. The essential point here is that they are generic, and the need within the school – and, more particularly, within the curriculum area – is to be much more precise and specific. The process for achieving this precision is practised to a greater or lesser degree in most schools but is worth outlining if only to facilitate comment on certain features:

a) The starting point must be *a clear philosophy or policy*, or, at the very least, an honest search for the information and guidance which will make the formation of such a policy quickly possible. Too many school in-service programmes in the past have resembled an educational blind man's buff in which what you touch is what you have. Such ill-planned and aimless programmes are unworthy of the profession and, thankfully, are now much less frequent since the introduction of Grant Related In-Service Training (now the Local Education Authority Training Grants Scheme). The delegation of financial control to schools will no doubt further concentrate the mind and discourage the serendipity approach.

b) Once the policy has been determined it is possible to *review and analyse* the current situation in the light of that policy.

c) Following the review and analysis the third stage requires the formation of *a development plan*, only one aspect of which will be the identification of an in-service programme, for the plan will also address other needs such as the provision of resources, both human (teachers and support staff) and material (physical accommodation, equipment, etc.). The in-service training component of the development plan should both state and prioritise needs, thus establishing a short-term, medium-term, and (provisional) long-term strategy.

It must be said that if there are still doubts and uncertainties regarding the expressive arts policy or if the policy has not been clearly articulated, this may represent the top priority training need. Indeed, it may be necessary to refer back to the establishing of aims for this area of experience, which we discussed in an earlier chapter.

d) The essential next step is to match the itemised training need with the *appropriate training style*. The range is wide indeed, but includes:

- *Secondments* Traditionally, secondments have tended to be associated with personal professional development and/or school need and have been of one-year or one-term duration. But increasingly LEAs are using targeted secondments which take a teacher from a school for a fixed period, usually to assist with the implementation of a new policy or curriculum initiative. The introduction of the National Curriculum is being accompanied by a proliferation of such secondments. A comparatively new phenomenon is the flexible secondment whereby a teacher is released for an agreed number of days per year – say twenty or thirty days – to undertake a specific task, usually at the behest of the LEA. The secondment continues to be an effective tool for curriculum change. Unfortunately, from the school's point of view, it also tends to be a route to higher and better places, and all too often secondees either fail to return or do so for only a short period of time before moving on.
- *Extended courses* Since secondments are now even more difficult to obtain than previously, an attractive alternative for acquiring new skills, or for updating earlier qualifications, is the extended course. The choice is extensive, ranging from courses provided by the Open University and higher education establishments to LEA 'twilight' or evening courses, or even weekend or vacation courses. Certainly there is a very real need for extended courses to address some of the issues discussed in this chapter – particularly those associated with the inadequacies of initial training. To provide a teacher with the competence and confidence to teach an arts discipline requires time. Isolated one-day sessions are no substitute.
- *The use of School and College focused In-service Teacher Education (SCITE) time* The essential characteristic of the Local Education Authority Training Grants Scheme funding (LEATGS) is that it puts the school firmly in charge of its own training funds, thereby facilitating a flexibility of usage previously unknown. For too long teachers had been prisoners in their own classrooms. It was possible to spend a lifetime in the profession without seeing any other teacher teach. Indeed, expressing the situation more accurately, it was difficult to contrive a situation

whereby a teacher could visit another school to observe a lesson being taught by another teacher – and in the training of expressive arts teachers the opportunity to observe process is crucial. The flexible use of SCITE time also enables schools to research more carefully curriculum innovations by seeking the experiences of others before they themselves tread the path.
- *Training days* The introduction of training days has stimulated both whole school and departmental discussions on a scale not previously experienced in most schools. In addition to the opportunity to discuss policy and planning, schools often use the time available to share skills in workshop situations, sometimes collaborating with other schools – often those in their particular cluster.
- *Residencies* The value of residencies as a vehicle for in-service training is discussed in another chapter. Suffice it to say here that it is a much underused method. To bring a professional artist into the 'classroom' situation introduces a new dimension – a catalyst for change.
- *Exchange* There is no doubt that the exchange of teachers between establishments has a great deal to offer – at least in theory. In practice it can prove difficult to organise on a part-time basis. By far the most effective exchanges have occurred when teachers have made a full-time exchange for a fixed period of time, varying from a week to a year. An alternative arrangement can sometimes be made to work where the exchange takes place on a one day per week basis.

e) The fifth stage is obviously the *actioning of the programme* followed by
f) the *evaluation*.

A further dimension of the development plan is the *time-scale*. The time-line should indicate the intended duration of the plan in its entirety but should also be divided into phases, each with its specific target. The total length of the plan is clearly a matter for the individual school to determine. It will almost certainly take more than one year, but plans which stretch beyond two years become increasingly speculative and of dubious value. There are too many variables to plan so far ahead. Quite apart from any other consideration, the speed of change is such that the goalposts seem to be constantly moving. The introduction of programmes of study and attainment targets, assessment and recording procedures, appraisal systems, changing priorities attached to Government funding, etc., all conspire to make long-term planning a precarious occupation. Thus in the present context 'long term' means anything more than two years ahead.

It is also necessary to build into the development plan opportunity for *feedback* and implementation. We frequently read of the *obligation* on teachers to report back on in-service activities. We seldom read of their *right* to report back. How often have teachers who have participated in stimulating in-service courses or events been frustrated by the lack of opportunity to share that experience with colleagues? Such frustration is extremely damaging to the teacher's morale and self-esteem – sometimes to the point where the teacher contributes less rather than more to the work of the school. If the school is serious about its in-service programme, it will appreciate that 'breathing space' is necessary for the impact of an activity to be absorbed. The need, or opportunity, to share the experience gives urgency to the process of analysing and evaluating the activity. It is also worth commenting that implementation following an in-service activity is much easier, and is more likely to succeed, if more than one teacher is involved in the initial activity. Although this suggestion may sound extravagant, it is usually true to say that the involvement of two teachers rather than one results in more than twice the value.

The role of the LEA

Whilst the emphasis has been upon the school identifying and actioning its own programme, it will nevertheless be looking to the LEA for guidance and assistance. Inspectors and advisers of the LEA are in a unique position to be aware of the needs of all of the schools and can often coordinate training programmes across the Authority. The school will look to the LEA on a number of issues, including:

a) The interpretation of information and legislation – accompanied, where necessary, by the provision of appropriate training programmes. The introduction of the GCSE provides a good example and, of course, the introduction of the National Curriculum will most certainly make similar demands. Often the voices from above are less prescriptive than they may seem at first, and one function of the advisory service is to indicate, and explore with teachers, a range of possible, imaginative responses. The present situation in which drama and dance are seemingly left out of the list of foundation subjects for the National Curriculum is a case in point. The fact is that they *are* present but are subsumed under other subject headings, i.e. English and physical education. It is a responsibility of advisers to make this point clear to schools and to illustrate ways in which the expressive arts subjects can be drawn together as a coherent group of disciplines. How a school chooses to deliver the curriculum is its own business, providing it fulfils the demands of the programmes of study and the accompanying attainment targets, but it must be able to look to the LEA for training programmes associated with, for example, assessment, testing and recording, as required for the National Curriculum.

b) The provision of courses in response to a widely expressed need. For example, the arts management courses mentioned above may represent a collective need in some Authorities, and certainly the need to provide a number of extended courses in lieu of inadequate initial training will be the experience of many. The demand for courses of this nature is encouraging LEAs to consult with neighbouring universities or other higher education establishments regarding possible forms of accreditation. Modular schemes are being devised for which credits can be gained, leading ultimately to a Certificate or Advanced Diploma. It is right and appropriate that additional qualifications should be accessible in this way for teachers who are prepared to undertake the prolonged period of study required. Certainly such schemes offer an effective way of enhancing initial qualifications.

c) The provision of a range of courses aimed at introducing new initiatives, learning styles, and so on. It is a responsibility of the LEA to lead as well as to respond.

d) The organisation of opportunities to meet and share experiences with other teachers.

e) The dissemination of good practice. Schools regularly ask to be referred to models of good practice, and yet such models are exceedingly difficult to find. Often it is the case that a school which is strong in one facet of arts work may be weak in others, and it is certainly true that a school may be regarded as progressive purely because it is one step ahead of the rest of the pack. There is an inherent danger that such a school may easily acquire a false impression of its own achievements.

f) Assistance with, and advice on, the development of structures capable of delivering an expressive arts curriculum.

g) Assistance from advisory teachers. Good advisory teachers are probably the most efficient form of in-service training and the most effective vehicle through which to implement change. The major problem is that there are generally too few of them. In consequence they either service a few schools well, to the neglect of a large number of other schools, or they service a large number of schools, which clearly means sacrificing quality for quantity.

Finding the teachers

The focus to this point has been very much concerned with improving the quality of the teachers we have, both by expecting and demanding that there will be better initial training, and by addressing in-service needs. But what happens if the teachers are not in the schools in the first place, or are not coming through? What happens if there is a shortage of expressive arts teachers? In many places such a shortage already exists. There are few specialist dance teachers, and the shortfall in music teachers will inevitably increase. In the absence of a steady supply of teachers of the right quality other strategies need to be explored.

A first step must clearly be to extend the sphere of influence of existing teachers. The practice of using curriculum leaders is well established in many primary schools and an investment in the development of this principle within the expressive arts would be money well spent. It is a process which maximises existing expertise and at the same time provides a network into which it is possible to inject new initiatives, learning styles and resources. There is, of course, no reason why the curriculum leader should be confined to one school. In a district or area where there is a shortage of specialist skills, the notion of a curriculum leader working with a cluster of schools has much to commend it. In rural areas with a proliferation of small schools, the advantages of a shared appointment are only too apparent. When the work of the curriculum leaders is supplemented by the provision of support groups which meet regularly to improve personal expertise and to extend classroom competence and confidence, there will be a structure for positive development. This will simultaneously disarm those critics who might otherwise view the process as a first-aid, or damage-limitation, exercise. Indeed out of necessity often emerges a more creative solution to a problem, if only because the routine response is impractical or obsolete and fresh thinking is required.

In the present context, fresh thinking means looking beyond the school gate and asking 'Who is there out there who can help?'. The short answer is 'We don't know!' but we can make an informed guess. There will be mothers who are trained teachers who have left the profession temporarily, or more permanently, because of family commitments. It is likely that there will be at least one practising artist. There will be other members of the community with artistic skills which would benefit the pupils in the school. What these people have in common is a shared disinclination to become full-time teachers, but that should not cause us therefore to overlook their value to the school as a resource. Once located, such a resource needs to be investigated fully to discover how it can most effectively and efficiently be used. This may well be on a restricted part-time basis or an occasional, intermittent pattern. That is fine, if it means that the learning experiences available to the pupils are enriched and the range of teaching and learning skills increased.

Changes in circumstances are going to demand much more flexibility than has characterised curriculum construction and staffing patterns in the past. In the chapter devoted to curriculum issues the suggestion was made that time-patterns and the uses of time need to be reviewed. Not all activities, even within a single subject discipline, benefit from an even distribution of time. The call for a review was made for educational reasons, but the need may be further underlined and made urgent by staffing difficulties. It may be easier to buy in a block of expertise over a short period of time to enrich a deprived area of the curriculum than to secure the services of a teacher or other specialist on a thin, drip-feed basis throughout the school year. The quality and lasting impact of an experience is more important for the pupil than any misguided argument (however well-intentioned) which suggests that if a subject cannot be taught regularly it should be excluded from the curriculum. Such thinking has caused pupils in some schools to be completely denied any form of music or dance teaching in recent years. This in no way conflicts with my comment elsewhere that an unsupported one-off artist residency can provide a recipe for frustration. Here I am suggesting that a programme of 'imported' patchwork provision is better than no provision at all. It is likely that the curriculum of the future will resemble a mosaic in which the individual pieces may well comprise a variety of shapes and colours but which collectively produce a coherent and comprehensible picture.

Such blocks of expertise, or blocks of experience, may be single or multi-disciplined. It remains to be seen whether LEAs will anticipate likely demands and create the necessary channels and structures. A starting point might be the targeted buying in, or bartering between schools, to cover a particular module or unit of work. Collaboration arrangements are not uncommon post-16 and may need to be extended. The LEA may elect to second a team of teachers, an expressive arts 'flying squad', whose services could be bought by schools, thereby reimbursing the LEA for the initial outlay, organisation and administration. Certainly if LEAs do not demonstrate a willingness to take a lead, it is probable that private 'consultancy' groups or agencies will step in.

The introduction of the Local Management of Schools with its associated delegated financial control will inevitably speed the demise of open-ended contracts and at the same time will make possible a whole range of alternatives, at the discretion of the headteacher and governors. Thus fixed-term contracts, job sharing and split contracts will become much more common. In the past it has not been easy, in response to changing needs, to convert a normal teaching contract into one which divided the teacher's workload evenly between daytime and evening adult/community education work. Similarly, traditional patterns of teacher employment have often seen a specialist dance teacher in one school spending a high proportion of her time teaching PE and games whilst at a neighbouring school a PE and games specialist struggled with dance! Schools will enjoy a new freedom and will have available a particularly powerful tool – the ability to hire and fire. The future of the expressive arts in our schools will depend not a little upon the vision of headteachers and governors, combined with the creative and responsible exercising of that new freedom, in all its forms.

CHAPTER 7 ARTISTS IN EDUCATION

The artist – all sorts and conditions of men

The stereotyped image of the professional artist has traditionally been less than flattering. He – for the image has mostly been masculine – has belonged to the race of the great unclean (being hirsute and of shabby appearance), has lived in conditions of extreme poverty in some dilapidated garret, has enjoyed an amoral or immoral lifestyle, and has behaved in a manner variously considered as eccentric, odd or reprehensible. He has often been accorded the reputation of being a subversive influence in society. In fairness, it is not difficult to produce a list of great artists across the arts whose lifestyles have given a degree of credence to the above description. But this romantic caricature has tended to increase the mystique of the arts and, in education, has served to exaggerate the tension between 'school' art and 'real' art. It has fanned the notion that you have to be 'different' to be a good artist.

So what is the reality? The qualities which all artists seem to share are first, the sensitivity, awareness and vision to interpret the world about them (and their feeling responses to that world) in a uniquely selective way which both illuminates and informs; and second, the eloquence and mastery of technique to share that interpretation with others. For many artists this desire to create, to form or to *per*form becomes the driving passion of their existence and matters more than worldly reward or financial security. Others, for a variety of personal reasons, do choose security, although there can remain a deep disappointment or disillusionment – a feeling of having been compromised by a society with different values. But it is not possible to generalise about artists, for the most common characteristic they share is their individuality.

Immense benefits can be gained from involving the professional artist in the educational process, at all ages and in a variety of ways. But, precisely because of the individuality referred to above, not all artists are suited to education work – perhaps by inclination, by temperament, by lack of appreciation of what is required or by lack of appropriate communication skills – and great care needs to be exercised when engaging an artist to work in the school context. But more of this later.

Why a residency?

Let us first consider why a residency might prove a valuable stimulus to the development of arts work in school:

a) Perhaps the most obvious and most immediate impact is one of novelty. For a group of pupils who have been accustomed to the same teacher over a period of time, the introduction of a 'new' face in itself generates change. It promotes an air of curiosity: a need to know more about the artist. And, of course, there is an added dimension if the artist is from a different culture. The pupil ponders, 'What does the person do exactly?', 'What is he or she like?', 'How is he or she different from the teacher?', 'Why is he or she here?', 'What is expected of me?'. It is worth commenting that the relationship between artist and pupil is often quite different from that between teacher and pupil, though the nature and quality of the changed relationship is something so individual that, again, it defies generalisation. Then, too, novelty is further emphasised if the residency is accompanied by any adjustment in lesson pattern – perhaps by creating an extended block of time. Such a rescheduling implies a sense of importance and underlines the fact that it is a special occasion. It should be recognised that the novelty of a residency extends beyond the classroom and often succeeds in giving the arts a higher profile both within the school and within the wider community.

b) The initial atmosphere of novelty is frequently superseded by a sense of awe and admiration evoked by the artist's professional skills. Most often it is technical accomplishment which first arouses this response, regardless of the art form. Thus a pupil will be impressed – perhaps inspired – by the dexterity of a violinist, the agility and quality of movement of a dancer or the sureness of touch of the artist painting on canvas. Gradually, as the residency unfolds, the artist is able to draw upon and extend the pupil's own skills, and will also seek to nurture the pupil's artistic and creative awareness as together they explore responses to, or interpretations of, a chosen stimulus.

c) An integral part of this professionalism is the need for rigour and discipline. Quality in artistic expression – whether in composition or performance – can only be achieved through meticulous preparation and an acceptance of nothing but the best. In the case of composition this may well involve detailed observation or research, and will certainly require drafting and redrafting, or the preparation of a range of preliminary sketches.

A short while ago I was associated with a school production of *Cavalleria Rusticana*, for which we engaged a professional set-designer to work with pupils on the set for the opera. In fact the designer, accustomed to the dimensions of the Royal Opera House, became so excited by the challenge of the constraints imposed by a school stage, that he set to and quite independently prepared his own design. Indeed he went much further, for he constructed a scale model of his design, accurate in every detail (just as would be required at the Royal Opera House). It is not difficult to appreciate that pupils and staff alike were left speechless when the design and the model appeared, for this was no 'backcloth and flats' but a three-dimensional construction of a Sicilian village square, realistic in every detail, using a variety of levels, excitingly angled walls and arches, with textured surfaces convincingly suggesting ageing, weathered stone. Their amazement was increased further when they saw the great sheaf of photographs and extracts copied from reference sources, together with countless preliminary sketches, which had provided an authentic basis for the final design. For a variety of reasons such detailed preparation and thoroughness is not a common feature of everyday life in most comprehensive schools, but what a priceless encounter it was for the pupils and teachers involved! They were able to understand the process in all its stages and, importantly, were able to be involved with the designer in the realisation and construction of the final set.

Similar examples could be recounted from each of the arts disciplines. In the performing arts pupils are initially surprised that a singer will not perform without first undertaking a series of warming-up exercises, or that dancers involved in a residency must find time to carry out their daily class routines. But the need for discipline and attention to detail makes sense when set against the context of the ultimate quality, and pupils will often more readily accept a demanding personal schedule – at least for the duration of the residency!

d) Then, too, it is helpful that the pupil should experience the 'human' face of the artist – particularly, perhaps, if the artist is more usually seen on the concert platform or across footlights. This strange phenomenon, 'the artist', shares common feelings and emotions. He or she laughs and jokes, just as the pupil does, and possibly responds in a similar way to everyday social issues. The artist is generally approachable, for he or she is not so firmly bound by such conventions as 'received' appearance and language which sometimes serve to determine a respectful distance between teacher and pupil, even in this enlightened age. To see the god in the flesh – devoid of grease paint and any other paraphernalia and trappings of his or her profession which add to the mystique and magic but set him or her apart from his or her public – reduced to life size, makes the art form not only more accessible in terms of understanding, but more possible in terms of achievement. If the artist can succeed, the pupil may feel that he or she too has a chance. In workshop situations artists are very willing to share their expertise and experiences with others and will readily 'think aloud', permitting some insight into their inner process. It is during such sessions that the pupil learns that the artist faces similar problems, has similar decisions to make and, indeed, is quite fallible and capable of making mistakes! Poets are particularly effective in heightening pupils' awarenesses, both of the world around them and of their own experiences and responses. Together, significant experiences or incidents are discussed, crystallised and encapsulated in poetic form, and the pupil is led to recognise that he or she and the poet not only inhabit the same world but often share the same realities.

e) Inspiration can occur when the pupil observes the work of an artist and experiences the strong feeling which says 'I want to do that'. But working closely with an artist during a residency can introduce a new richness to this experience. To use an analogy familiar to all who have played any form of sport, even at a modest level, it is a common phenomenon that participating in a game with players whose ability is greater than your own has the effect of lifting your own performance well beyond its normal level, perhaps even beyond the standard of which you considered yourself capable. This is equally true in the expressive disciplines and, perhaps, particularly so in the performing arts where the pupil can reach unprecedented heights of achievement so exhilarating that, once tasted, this new dimension of experience will not be denied.

f) A characteristic of such inspirational occasions is that there is frequently little if any verbal communication between the performers. Numerous references have been made to the osmosis process in arts teaching, but here is something more. There develops an exciting chemistry between artist and pupil during which the vocabulary for communication is provided solely by the art form itself. Of course, such moments are very special and very rare, and I would not wish to give the impression that they represent a feature common to all residencies. But they can, and do, occur – given the essential ingredient of adequate time for artist and pupils to work together.

g) Very few artists are also trained teachers, although many have considerable experience of working in schools and other educational contexts. A lack of specialist training, combined with the unfamiliar constraints on resources and time, can initially pose problems for the artist (and for the teacher!), and recently the Arts Council and the Regional Arts Associations have given serious thought to the provision of training programmes for artists undertaking educational work. But such well-intentioned schemes could prove counter-productive. It is important to focus on the particular and highly developed skills the artist has rather than to be over-sensitive to possible pedagogic inadequacies. The artist is engaged as an artist, the teacher as a teacher. An awareness of each other's role is essential, but to assume an interchange of skills is unrealistic and undesirable. The artist brings a freshness of approach – I am tempted to suggest an innocence. He or she is there for a fixed, brief period of time, and carries no preconceived ideas of what pupils cannot do, either in terms of artistic vision or through persistence and graft. In his or her innocence he or she expects high standards and frequently gets them by making demands which the regular teacher would have difficulty in pursuing. I can recall numerous occasions when writers have required four, five or six redrafts and pupils have obliged without demur, to the amazement (and sometimes consternation) of their teachers. Similarly the long periods of sustained concentration demanded of young dancers have been quite staggering.

It would be sad if, in introducing artists to the craft of the classroom, we also made them aware of the impossible! Let us preserve their innocence.

h) It is not difficult to accept that residencies by artists contribute significantly to closing the perceived gap between 'school' art and 'real' art, and provide a smooth and natural introduction to the professional repertoire. Having met the artist, the pupil associates with him or her and adopts a sense of ownership. The pupil wants to see 'his' or 'her' artist perform professionally. It may be argued that this is not the most convincingly legitimate of reasons for a young person to take an interest in the arts. But I would suspect that for most of us our initial interest was ignited by some equally advantageous accident – perhaps by fortuitous home circumstances or the contagious enthusiasm of a particular teacher. The important point is that, by whatever route, each individual should at some time be granted the opportunity of encountering 'live' art of the highest possible quality and in surroundings and circumstances which appropriately enhance the experience and the occasion. To meet the artist is a rare privilege.

Planning a residency

The characteristics described may not all appear in every residency, but it would be an unfortunate and badly planned residency which failed to demonstrate substantial evidence of the positive relationships and features outlined. Since preparation is so important to a successful residency it will be helpful to examine the process in some detail. There are effectively five stages:

a) *Why?*

There are many horror stories which circulate among artists relating to occasions when they have arrived at a school only to discover that they were not expected and, in some instances, were not welcome. Such engagements have usually proved to be the product of a phone call from some benevolent officer of the LEA or the Regional Arts Association suggesting to the headteacher of the school that it would be a 'good thing' to take advantage of a prestigious offer he or she is about to make. The headteacher, unaccustomed to being the receiver of unsolicited largesse, instinctively accepts, perhaps without undertaking the necessary consultation processes with the teachers concerned. Such ill-conceived ventures have no place in the present discussion other than to illustrate what should *not* be done.

A planned residency will begin with the question 'why?' – for the residency should be arranged in response to an identified need. It might be used to stimulate a planned programme, to bring a new dimension to work already begun or to provide a fitting climax to the programme. It might be used to provide a skill in which the teacher feels unsure or inadequate, or in which he or she would simply welcome the opportunity to work alongside the professional to extend his or her personal expertise. Many residencies – indeed, most – have an incidental in-service component, the value of which can easily be underestimated. There is a major advantage in bringing the artist into the school, and into the 'real' situation, where he or she is faced with the same pupils and the same constraints that the teacher meets daily. One in-school residency can be as valuable as a cluster of simulated workshops on courses unimaginatively presented in an environment which has never been sullied by mischievous grins and dirty shoes. An aware teacher may ask questions of the artist's pedagogic style but will, at the same time, store away many ideas, professional wrinkles and skills which can be developed and personalised for future use.

I am suggesting, then, that there can be any number of legitimate reasons why a teacher could consider a residency to be valuable to the teaching process. I would also stress that the response to the question 'Why?' should be precise rather than general, and that the reason given should reflect an identified need and should be rooted in an ongoing development programme.

b) *Focus*

If the reasons for the residency have been clearly thought through, this stage in the process is really one of fine-tuning. Specific aims need to be set down, and thought given to the expected, or hoped-for, outcome.

For the teacher organising a first residency there is always the temptation to be over-ambitious, both in terms of what can be achieved and also the number of pupils to be involved. But quality must take precedence over quantity – particularly if the impact of the residency is to have any long-term benefits. In practice this means that the aims should be few, and that the emphasis should be on depth rather than on breadth. Similarly, whilst it is understandable that the teacher should be anxious to stretch an expensive and rare resource as far as possible, and to give the maximum number of pupils an opportunity to meet the artist, it must be appreciated that that is precisely what the pupils would be doing – i.e. meeting the artist rather than gaining a meaningful experience. Such an arrangement is a false economy.

It is more effective and rewarding for the artist to work with one group four times than to work with four groups once each. By working with the same group on a number of occasions, there is opportunity for artist and pupils to become acquainted and for a programme of work to be developed and perhaps completed to the greater satisfaction of all the participants – pupils, artist and teacher. Also, the beneficial characteristics identified earlier in the chapter seldom occur instantly. They need time and space to develop and grow.

c) *Who?*

The next step in the process is to find an artist who is able to address the established aims. As has already been indicated, not all artists are suited to education work – and those who are often have preferences regarding the nature of the projects they will undertake. Some will work only with small groups of the most able pupils, others prefer large, mixed-ability groups. Some work with concepts and skills most frequently found in the upper secondary years, others prefer to work with the less inhibited primary age range. Some are larger-than-life extroverts, robust in character and, perhaps, 'careless' in their choice of vocabulary. Others are quiet introverts who communicate most eloquently through their art. There is no shortage of artists. The crucial problem is how to find the right one: how to achieve the right match. Fortunately there are numerous sources the teacher can use:

- *The LEA Advisory Services*
  It is unlikely that the teacher will be the first in the Authority to promote a residency, and there may already be in existence a bank of information relating to artists who have previously worked with schools. It is also possible that the Authority may have funds available to support such a venture. In all events a telephone call to the appropriate Inspector/Adviser can do no harm.
- *The Regional Arts Association*
  Each area of the country has its own Regional Arts Association and each RAA has a directory of artists who work in the region. Indeed, the directory may well extend beyond the local region. Whilst such a directory may seem to offer a solution to the problem, it can more easily prove to be a recipe for disaster. It will include all artists – not only those accustomed to education

work – and is unlikely to give the detailed information necessary for matching purposes. It is unwise to select from such a directory solely on the grounds of the artist's specialism. A far more effective use can be made of the RAA by telephoning the appropriate officer, i.e. the music officer or drama officer etc. These officers are generally quite knowledgeable about the artists who work within their sphere and will be only too happy to provide the sort of additional profile information essential to the selection process. They will often be able to list schools where the artist has worked previously. Wherever possible, such contacts should be followed up by a telephone call since the fact that an artist carried out a residency in a school is in itself no guarantee that the residency was successful. Such research is necessary if the right artist is to be found. We do not employ teachers purely on the grounds that they have taught before. We need evidence of a track record.

- *Organisations with Education Units*

  The Commonwealth Institute has an extensive list of Commonwealth artists covering most art forms. For the most part these artists are well used to working in schools and there is good back-up support available through the outreach workers from the Institute. In addition, the Institute possesses a fine collection of resource materials which can be loaned or hired.

  For some years now companies in receipt of subsidies from the Arts Council have been required, in return, to invest a small percentage of their income in educational projects. Thus major opera, theatre and dance (both ballet and contemporary) companies, as well as art galleries, have education officers and promote education programmes. Initially such work was often undertaken with reluctance but, largely through the imaginative work of the education officers, companies have begun to appreciate the potential of such diversification and the level of commitment has risen considerably. These units are now a rich source of supply for artist residencies, and teachers should not be deterred by the clichéd, highbrow images associated with some of these art forms. Things are not always what they seem! It is an essential task of the education officers to provide programmes which penetrate the barriers of prejudice and there is ample evidence to confirm that they are succeeding. Consider, for example, the extent to which schools' matinées are oversubscribed at the Royal Opera House, both for the opera and ballet programmes; or the quite staggering success of the Sadlers Wells Royal Ballet Company working in the Handsworth district of Birmingham – an area remembered for the riots of a few years ago – with adolescents, mostly male and mostly of Commonwealth extraction. The officers positively enjoy the challenge of shattering illusions, and several companies, like the London Contemporary Dance Theatre, have programmes which cater for pupils with special needs. Frequently projects seem to step some distance away from the original art form and the link may seem tenuous, or at least not immediately obvious. For example, Kent Opera, shortly before their demise, produced a project on 'Film, Drama and Music', during which pupils analysed the relationship between film and music in silent movies then, under the guidance of a team of professionals – comprising a film-maker, a silent film musician, a composer and a producer – created their own short film with music. Gradually the similarities between this exercise and the writing and structuring of an opera were made apparent.

So many companies, the length and breadth of the country, are now offering programmes that to attempt to do justice to them would require a separate volume. Once again, a telephone call to any company or gallery, asking to speak to the education officer, will be sufficient to discover what the company can offer. Most companies with a developed education programme will produce literature outlining a range of 'off-the-peg' projects or packages. These may not suit the teacher's particular needs, in which case the teacher should discuss with the education officer the opportunities for creating a 'bespoke' residency. Artists and officers are generally both versatile and accommodating and welcome such an invitation, particularly if they can be involved in the planning from an early stage. The teacher should also recall that at this stage he or she is in search of an artist who can respond to an identified need, and should not be distracted from that quest by the lure of other offers which may be more appropriate to other needs on other occasions. (In this context it is important to note the distinction between programmes which are ongoing and those which are associated with a touring exhibition or performance and are therefore ephemeral.)

- An attraction of working with the Education Units is that again it is possible to verify the nature and quality of what is on offer.

But there are also other agencies specializing in educational work, such as the Firebird Trust at Nottingham which deals essentially with music projects. Similarly the Poetry Society, the National Poetry Secretariat and the Book Trust produce lists of poets and writers. Theatre in Education groups often welcome independent approaches outside their normal contracted programmes. The Craft Council may also be able to assist where appropriate.
- Yet another source may be a local higher education establishment. Many colleges have specialist staff, or contact with professional artists. The colleges enjoy the possibility of linking with other educational groups – and with potential markets.
- The teacher may, of course, locate an artist without reference to any organisation, association or agency – perhaps through personal acquaintance. Increasingly schools are drawing upon their own immediate community for pockets of expertise. If the required match can be made in this way and the teacher feels reasonably confident that the desired quality of experience is likely to ensue, such an arrangement is to be encouraged – not least because follow-up work could be readily available and accessible.

It is opportune at this point to alert the teacher to other schemes and programmes which may not directly answer the immediate problem but which may sow seeds and offer contacts for future reference. I have in mind particularly the work of such organisations as the Arts Council of Great Britain and the British Film Institute. Both the ACGB and the BFI identify and fund specific initiatives, such as residencies by professional photographers or media workers. The ACGB is the parent body of the Regional Arts Associations, and contact with the local RAA will provide information relating to current and forthcoming initiatives. The BFI has its own education officer. Both organisations have substantial resource banks available for educational use.

d) *Funding/Conditions/Organisation*

Although most residencies which are properly planned and organised offer good value for money – particularly when the INSET dimension is taken into consideration – they are not cheap, and one fears for the future as schools assume responsibility for their own finances. Unenlightened governors and senior management teams may take a great deal of persuading before they are able to appreciate the value of such ventures. Certainly it is likely that in many instances schools will need to look beyond their own resources for assistance with funding. Most of the recognised sources have already been mentioned in passing – the LEA, the RAA, the possibility of participating in special initiatives organised by the Arts Council or the BFI. Of these the RAA may well prove to be the most useful, first, because they have a major responsibility to support local artists, and second, because most Associations operate a shared funding policy as one method of exercising this responsibility. It is undoubtedly much easier to secure matching funding than it is to obtain the full cost of a residency from any source. On occasions the sharing of a residency with a neighbouring school can help.

A number of national companies, such as Marks & Spencer and W H Smith, provide funding on a fairly regular basis, but most of the major businesses and banks prefer their arts sponsorship to be associated with rather more prestigious events than a residency in a local school.

Having located the artist and secured the necessary funding, initial arrangements are often discussed by telephone. Even at the preliminary stage these discussions need to encompass such practical details as the size of groups, the ability range, the age range, the length of time with each group including the number of sessions, the facilities and equipment available, agreement on fees and other expenses, and clearly stated dates and times. Most important, the aims of the residency should be discussed and agreement reached regarding the desired outcome. If agreement cannot be reached on this latter point, the discussion should be terminated and an alternative artist sought. On the small number of occasions when residencies fail or disappoint, the most common cause of failure is lack of clarity concerning the aims of the residency. Once agreement has been reached, the teacher should write to the artist confirming all arrangements. If it is felt necessary to secure a contract, a second copy can be enclosed for the artist to sign and return as an acknowledgement of the agreed terms.

When the residency takes place, a teacher should be present at all times. The artist is not a surrogate teacher and, quite apart from the considerable INSET advantages referred to above, the teacher has a legal responsibility for the pupils.

e) *Follow-up*

Unless the impact of a residency can be satisfactorily sustained, it should not be undertaken. A residency without follow-up is a recipe for frustration. Such a statement may sound platitudinous but it is not uncommon, for example, for a school without a dance teacher to promote a dance residency in an attempt to redress the deficiency. The result is that having had the appetite for dance whetted by the enthusiasm and expertise of professional artists, the pupils feel frustrated and cheated when the school cannot provide continued tuition. The situation is made worse rather than better.

Levels of understanding: the 'five-star system'

During the course of this chapter several references have been made to the role of the artist in residence as a bridge between 'school' art and 'real' art, and also as an introduction to the professional repertoire. Experience in working with artists over a number of years has led me to believe that it is possible to construct a diagram which shows some correlation between the level of artist involvement and the nature of a pupil's understanding of a particular art form. I am not for one moment suggesting that a deep appreciation is only possible as a result of artist intervention. That would be utter nonsense. But I am convinced that in many cases the process leading to understanding and appreciation can be accelerated and the experience enriched through contact with the professional artist. The level of enrichment is dependent upon the nature and extent of that contact, and can be crudely represented by the method used to denote the octane level in petrol, i.e. a star system! (See diagram overleaf.)
LEVEL ONE (*)
This respresents a very basic level of knowledge and understanding of an art form and comprises particularly the accumulation of information both factual and anecdotal, useful and entertaining. In some instances teachers have given as much attention to the biographical detail of the artist as to the work he or she produced and, indeed, knowledge about specific works has not necessarily been accompanied by an acquaintance with the works themselves. At best, pupils have been directed towards sound recordings, or minute reproductions of great paintings. In many schools, generations of pupils have studied prescribed plays without having set foot inside a theatre. Often the attraction of this style of teaching/learning is that it can be tested and marked. There is an identifiable body of knowledge: facts to be learned.

LEVELS OF UNDERSTANDING

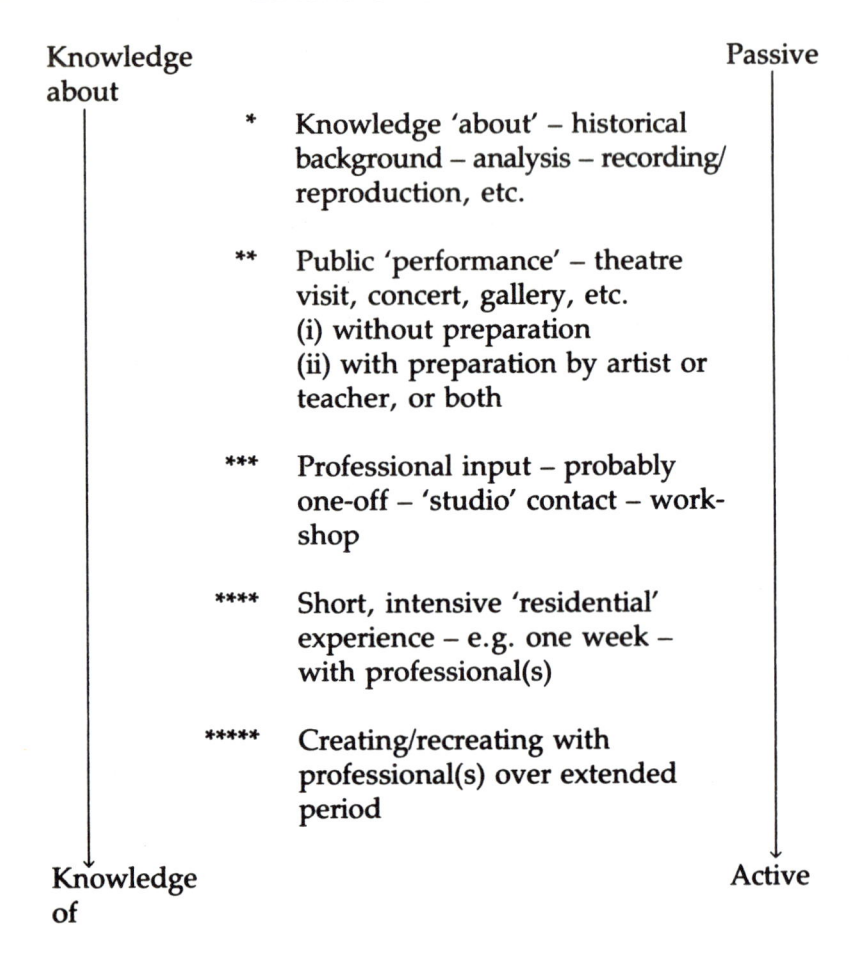

Knowledge about   Passive

*   Knowledge 'about' – historical background – analysis – recording/reproduction, etc.

**   Public 'performance' – theatre visit, concert, gallery, etc.
(i) without preparation
(ii) with preparation by artist or teacher, or both

***   Professional input – probably one-off – 'studio' contact – workshop

****   Short, intensive 'residential' experience – e.g. one week – with professional(s)

*****   Creating/recreating with professional(s) over extended period

Knowledge of   Active

Indeed so many facts have been needlessly absorbed that modern generations have been embarrassed by the mountain of redundant intellectual clutter and have spawned a proliferation of quiz games, typified at one extreme by television's University Challenge and at the other by the more honestly labelled Trivial Pursuits!

Of course background knowledge is helpful in any area of study, providing it is used as just that – as a stepping-stone leading to meaningful contact with the subject of the study. Unfortunately, in the past that target has often not been reached, and the accumulation and regurgitation of factual knowledge has become an end in itself. Enlightened attitudes towards learning, and vastly improved means of accessibility to 'live' sources, could soon render such a criticism obsolete. Much will depend on how schools use their financial independence, and on the level of priority attached to visits etc.

LEVEL TWO (**)

This level presents the pupil with the opportunity for true contact with the art form. It involves a visit to the gallery, the theatre, the concert hall, and allows the work to speak directly. The impact of such an experience is often unforgettable and incalculable. The pupil gasps with surprise at the size and vibrancy of a painting, so inadequately represented in the reference book. Sounds in the concert hall have an exhilarating richness, and there are suddenly many more dimensions than expected to this holistic experience. And is there anything more magical than the first visit to the theatre to look in on that other world beyond the footlights? Knowledge gathered at Level One now acquires a context, and illuminates the new experience.

Even within Level Two, what the pupil takes from the live encounter is likely to be significantly influenced by the quantity and quality of the preparation. The inexperienced young visitor may be so overwhelmed by the general impact that his or her attention flits excitedly from one aspect to another without really registering anything in depth. Whilst it is possible to offer some sympathy with this approach, it is probable that the teacher could enhance the meaningfulness of the occasion by directing attention towards specific facets. Certainly pupils find pre-performance sessions with actors and/or other company members most beneficial, and there is evidence that companies are increasingly responding to this need, particularly for matinée performances. Many galleries offer a parallel service.

Such can be the impact of the live encounter that some teachers believe if only a visit can be engineered, all will be well. There will be an action replay of the road to Damascus! Conversions will abound. But, of course, an energy which has the power to convert also has the power to divert, and if a mistake is made there may well not be an opportunity for the teacher to try again. This underlines the need not only for adequate preparation but also for the exercising of great care regarding the choice of programme and its appropriateness to the pupils' present level of experience.

LEVEL THREE (***)

Level Three represents the oldest pattern of residency which typically involved a visiting children's writer who, during the course of a half day, would talk to several groups of pupils about being a writer and about his or her books in particular. This style of writer's residency, though still used, is perhaps on the wane in favour of the extended residency, but the one-session visit provides a format well suited to the needs of the touring companies – theatrical, operatic, dance or orchestral. And, without wishing to overstate the case, it should be recognised that this arrangement is better suited to the needs of the writers and the companies than to the needs of the pupils. Of course they have a value, and of course pupils on occasion are inspired by such visits. But often the visits are designed as much for promotional as for educational purposes.

There is, however, a very much more effective way of using the one-off professional visit. For maximum effect a confined space such as a studio is preferable. The number of pupils should be limited and the emphasis should be on pupil participation rather than purely as members of an audience. A studio-type setting generates considerable atmosphere, heightened by the close proximity of the artist. An extended session of this kind offers the opportunity for the pupil to understand more deeply the medium, and to experience some of the techniques necessary to explore and use its expressive qualities. It is also possible to focus on a particular aspect, to question and to seek alternative interpretations. A number of schools with whom I have contact have, for the past two years, organised sessions in which a professional actor has worked with 'A' Level English students, exploring Shakespeare texts, in the workshop style outlined. So successful have the sessions been that similar workshops have been structured to study Chaucer. The quality of experience made accessible through the single studio workshop session should not be underestimated.

LEVEL FOUR (****)

If the possibility exists to extend the workshop beyond just the one session then, of course, new opportunities are introduced. In particular it becomes possible for artist(s) and pupils together to create or recreate a reasonably complete piece of work. It may lack polish if measured by performance standards, but the exciting process of developing ideas and drawing them together can approach fruition. Most important, with the additional time available, the pupil is able to become absorbed in the activity and in the experience.

A typical residency at this level might involve the artist(s) working in a school for a week. Of course if the week is divided into a sequence of one-off sessions, little advantage is gained. An effective format involves intensive work with either one or two small groups, with some additional opportunity arranged for limited contact with others. This pattern is favoured by companies, particularly dance companies, but is adaptable to any of the disciplines.

LEVEL FIVE (*****)

The extended residency is one in which artist(s) and pupils work together at regular intervals over a long period, such as a term or more. The opportunities for such residencies are decidedly rare but the advantages are very considerable and justify the exercising of persistence, ingenuity and perhaps entrepreneurial skills! Quite apart from all else, sustained contact with an artist is far more likely to produce a lasting influence within the school.

But there are two other features of the diagram which are significant and require comment. The first is the continuum from 'passive' to 'active' understanding and appreciation which occurs during the progression from Level One to Level Five: from the one-star to the five-star experience. It is an obvious, yet very important phenomenon. The second is a parallel continuum progressing from 'knowledge about' to 'knowledge of': from information about, to experience of. The difference is fundamental and the journey is long. Yet that journey needs, at the very least, to be attempted if the pupil is to be given the opportunity of a meaningful understanding of an art form. A balanced arts diet should ideally contain elements of all five levels. Sadly, many pupils still leave secondary school without even experiencing Level Two.

Finally, contact with the professional artist can do much to eliminate artifically created categories of 'school' art and 'real' art, 'pop' art and 'high' art, and can remove once and for all the notion that some art forms are elitist and inaccessible. Misconceptions abound and thrive largely on ignorance and ill-informed prejudice. Artist residencies have the capacity not only to refute the unjust and the untrue but, more important, to replace scepticism with enthusiasm. The stereotyped images and clichéd attitudes of the past have no place in the arts curriculum of the 1990s.

CHAPTER 8 TOWARDS A POLICY FOR THE ARTS

Why a policy?

It is reasonable to begin by asking the question since many schools (probably most schools) have coped for a very long time without a stated policy for the arts. That does not necessarily mean that a policy has not existed. Often the 'undeclared' policy has been very evident in the ethos of the school, where it may have reflected the inspirational and charismatic qualities of an individual teacher or group of teachers – or, conversely, where an absence of expressive and creative work has indicated the low esteem attached to the arts disciplines. But traditions of 'ad hockery' which may have been adequate in the past are likely to be decidedly inadequate in a changed educational climate. The introduction of the National Curriculum and the Local Management of Schools has caused, and is causing, all involved in education to rethink existing practices. The circle of habit has been broken and has been replaced by a star of challenge. I reaffirm my belief that in this changed climate the opportunities for the arts are considerable, providing the case is argued with conviction rather than with apology and that it contributes to a clear policy for the arts.

There are essentially four reasons why a policy is needed:

a) A curriculum area requires shape and direction. Without shape, there is a lack of coherence and a likelihood of fragmentation. What the pupil receives may then depend on chance rather than planned entitlement. There is also a probability of overlapping programmes and duplicated resources. Without direction, there is difficulty in identifying achievement. How can you know when you have arrived if you don't know where you're going?

b) The expressive arts are not an island unto themselves but form part of the whole curriculum. Those with responsibility for overall curriculum management will wish to address matters of curriculum balance and interrelationship. They can only accomplish this if the component elements are well formed.

c) The Local Management of Schools cannot be efficiently and effectively undertaken with regard to the expressive arts without a clear arts policy. Those responsible for administrating and allocating funding need to know what is required. They have a right to expect the case to be justified.

d) All within the school (particularly pupils and teachers) *need* to be clear what the expressive arts are 'about' – what the policy is. Those outside the school (parents, governors, LEA, HMI, the general public) have a *right* to know.

Philosophy, understanding and aims

The foundation for a policy must be established through sound philosophy and understanding, and if that foundation is to be firm the debate must be thorough. There are teachers who seem to find such discussion embarrassing, almost as if it represented an invasion of their privacy. There are others who consider any query relating to their discipline to be audacious. And there are many who would rather 'get on with the job'. Such attitudes merely serve to underline the need for debate, they do not remove it. There are, of course, many others – a majority – who will relish the opportunity for the exchange and sharing of ideas, opinions and beliefs. It is certainly the case that there can be no short-cut, for much depends upon the outcome of the deliberations.

If the policy is to acquire credibility in the eyes of all, the range of consultation will need to be wide. At the core will be the group of teachers identified in an earlier chapter on the curriculum – that is, those directly involved in the delivery of an expressive arts curriculum (both taught and hidden) on a daily basis – but surrounding the core there will be other teachers, advisers, pupils, parents and governors. It is the interaction between these various interests which will increase understanding and promote a sense of ownership. A further circle of possible contributors whose opinions could be counselled on specific matters might include practising artists, officers of the Regional Arts Association, the Youth Service, Adult Education and appropriate members of the local community. The common characteristic of this group is that they all have something to offer to the arts in the school either through expertise, service or varied experience, and their invited comments may well enrich and inform debate. It is certainly not envisaged that the process should be conducted in some vast plenary gathering, but rather that small groups with shared interests should meet to discuss issues, with opportunities for overlap between the groups both to sharpen the focus and provide coherence. Thus it would be helpful to involve representatives of the governing body in staff discussions from time to time, and for representative arts staff to attend a governors' meeting to make a presentation or to provide information and offer a response to a specific agenda item. Liaison with the Parent Teachers' Association provides a similar opportunity for listening and informing, and the considerable parental representation on governing bodies could provide the sort of overlap referred to above. Whilst the thrust of the debate must rightly and properly be spearheaded by the professionals, the involvement of the lay representatives must be real if suspicion and ignorance are to be dismissed and understanding promoted. With the introduction of LMS it is important to recognise where the influence and power will reside.

The first task will be to establish a common language and shared understanding. Repeatedly, in earlier chapters, references have been made to ill-founded misconceptions about the arts, to prejudices and beliefs based on outdated personal experience, and to narrow interpretations of the term 'arts experience' reflecting the limited horizons associated with expressive arts education in the grammar schools. Sadly these attitudes are often held by those who mean well and think they understand! A similar difficulty can exist among arts teachers themselves or, to be more precise, among those isolationists who have no wish to leave their bunkers and face the world outside. By comparison, the philistine element on the governing body or on the PTA presents little problem. The enemies are often friends! It is for such reasons that the terminology should be clearly defined and agreed, negative anecdotal 'evidence' discouraged, and the slate wiped clean of any possible misunderstandings and clutter at the earliest possible opportunity. *The purpose of the consultations must be to build a new policy, not to tinker around with existing tradition and custom.*

The second point to clarify, and upon which agreement is necessary, is that the expressive arts in school are primarily concerned with the *educational function* of the arts rather than the social function. That is, they are about the acquisition of attitudes and skills which provide access to an essential area of experience unreachable by any other means: another way of knowing. From this will no doubt emanate discussion on the education of the senses, the education of feeling, awareness, symbol systems, and so on. There is ample material in earlier chapters to fuel the debate.

It will then be helpful to discuss the *aims* for arts education in school. The need to establish aims as a prelude to the construction of an arts curriculum has already been clearly stressed and it is important to introduce this topic to a wider audience. There is an additional point, that aims and objectives need to be reviewed regularly both to refresh the memory and to re-examine their relevance to changing circumstances.

A statement of entitlement

The consultation process should culminate in *a statement of entitlement for all pupils* – including those who by age or ability fall outside the statutory requirements of the National Curriculum. The TVEI extension 'curriculum of entitlement' itemises 'aesthetic' among a list of curriculum areas to be provided for post-16 students, but the interpretation and delivery are left as a local issue to be determined by schools and LEAs. Often, pupils with special educational needs make immense strides in personal growth through the expressive arts. For these pupils, direct 'feeling' communication makes accessible a 'real' world, a world from which they are not excluded, whether through mental or physical disability. The mainstream itself will, of course, comprise a very wide range of abilities. What is the entitlement of these pupils – *all* of them? The National Curriculum requirements must obviously be observed, but those requirements alone will provide only the tent poles without the canvas.

The statement of entitlement will be concerned with the *what* rather than with the *how*, but at the same time its authors must consider the realities of the world in which the decisions are being made and must be aware of the implications for delivery. If the school decides that all pupils are entitled to tuition on a musical instrument, what is the availability of instruments? What is the availability of tuition? It is likely that the statement would require a number of riders before such a commitment could be fulfilled. Similarly, consideration should be given not only to the provision for skill acquisition but also to experience enrichment opportunities including, for example, visits and artist residencies, but the restrictions regarding the costs which can legitimately be passed on to parents may well inhibit or constrain schools from including such highly desirable activities as an entitlement for all. There is no doubt that reverberations between the ideal and the practical will persist throughout the whole period during which the statement is being prepared, and beyond. But it is important that schools should settle for nothing less than the ambitious. The essential feature of the statement is that it must be *positive*, saying quite clearly what *is* the entitlement, not what is not.

Resourcing

The creation of a set of aims together with the statement of entitlement will inform, and provide a basis for, two further areas of policy: resourcing and organisation. (The latter will be considered later.) The quality of the discussions and the persuasive impact of the case argued will be all important if the level of resourcing is to be sufficient to meet requirements. That persuasive impact must convince a wide audience with varied interests and tastes. In particular it must persuade those who control the funding. It will serve little purpose for the consultation process to comprise a cosy chat between the converted if the people who hold the purse strings are elsewhere and are plainly not converted.

It will be acknowledged that they (senior managers, governors, etc.) have an unenviable task – that of apportioning funding and allocating resources in relation to the whole curriculum. If the policy for the arts is to fulfil its intended function in assisting that process it must not only outline a framework but must also spell out, where appropriate, the implied costs. These costs should be itemised and considered under broad budget headings such as staffing, accommodation, equipment/materials and miscellaneous. It is not suggested that the costing should be undertaken in detail. The purposes are twofold: first, to help middle managers and others realise that a request for another teacher is a request for an expensive resource and for a significant increase in funding and, second, to provide a tangible framework which can be quantified and thereby ratified as the accepted cost of the school arts policy.

It is worth repeating that the initial discussions should not be regarded as an unnecessary academic exercise. The nature of the debate needs to enthuse as well as persuade intellectually. Recall the earlier quotation from Abbs: *'Emotion gives knowledge motion'*. It is how people *feel* about the arts, as well as what they think, that matters. And enthusiasm is infectious.

Staffing

Staffing is clearly the single most expensive item for most curriculum areas and there may well be a tension between what the school wishes to provide and what it can afford to provide. The discussions leading to the statement of entitlement will no doubt have covered the first half of this equation, and may well have considered also desirable and workable staffing ratios. It is then for senior management to decide whether the needs can be balanced or whether adjustments need to be made. All curriculum areas have similar problems, of course, and one legitimate concern associated with the late positioning of the arts on the National Curriculum agenda is that concessions may have been made to core subjects and other foundation subjects which restrict the manoeuvrability of, and provision for, the expressive arts. This is not a plea for special treatment for the arts; it is an acknowledgement of the fact that in some schools the arts may not be starting off on an equal footing.

A further decision will relate to the range of specialisms to be provided, and how they will be provided. It seems likely that staffing patterns for the future will be more flexible than past arrangements, probably with job-sharing, split contracts, part-time teaching etc., complementing a central core of full-time permanent staff. Certainly there are strong arguments to support such a structure, and many would subscribe to the view that a part-time specialist has more to contribute than a classroom teacher offering their second or third subject. But at the moment such suggestions are speculation. What is important is that the school has a policy which it pursues to the best of its ability. For example, if it is decided that dance should be among the specialisms offered, then every attempt should be made to ensure that a dance programme is provided, and the fact that Miss Fairweather, who teaches PE, prefers hockey is not an adequate reason for allowing dance to disappear from the curriculum. At the very least, alternative ways of fulfilling the dance commitment need to be explored.

One option will be to provide Miss Fairweather with appropriate in-service training. The policy for the arts should comment on – and the Local Education Authorities Training Grant Scheme budget provides for – the professional development of the teacher. The expressive arts area will wish to secure its share of the training budget, and the enhancement of existing expertise and retraining to meet changed needs are proper uses of that funding. Indeed it is desirable for there to be an expressive arts in-service strategy procedure which identifies needs and appropriate training programmes.

Depending upon local circumstances, it may also be necessary for the school to have a statement within the arts policy relating to the employment and use of peripatetic staff.

Accommodation

The provision of appropriate accommodation for the arts can result only from an awareness of the need accompanied by the will to achieve what is possible, bearing in mind inevitable financial constraints. The Gulbenkian Report comments: *'Laboratories not only provide the facilities for scientific work, they provide a setting and a mood for it. Equally, the drama room, the art and music rooms facilitate expressive work partly through becoming associated with it'.*

In some instances provision is so inadequate that nothing short of a major building programme can satisfactorily address the problem. But in every school the task will be to ensure that best use is made of the available accommodation to meet the needs of the agreed curriculum aims. This will include:

- Recognising the importance of specialist accommodation for all disciplines, including drama and dance. The opportunity to use lights, for example, can completely transform drama lessons. But a list of reasons justifying specialist accommodation would be long indeed.
- Recognising that needs change, and that accommodation which may have been luxurious in the 1960s could be totally inadequate in the 1990s. Perhaps the most obvious change of direction has occurred in music where there is often a need for a number of small spaces for individual and group work, supported by suitable recording facilities including, ideally, a recording studio. Such arrangements are often desirable for classwork and are well nigh essential for GCSE coursework.
- Recognising that coherence between the arts is impeded if the accommodation provided for the disciplines is separated geographically. In such circumstances the declared curriculum and organisational aims and the location of the various arts disciplines will clearly be in conflict.

The costs associated with these three aspects of specialist accommodation will vary enormously from one school to another, as will the capacity to implement change.

A fourth aspect, relating to the quality of the school environment generally – including the ambience and the nature and quality of work displayed – will be common to all. The policy should acknowledge the ability of the environment to enhance the atmosphere in which learning takes place, and funding should be allocated to maintain the desired quality.

Equipment and materials

Schools have traditionally had the responsibility for distributing capitation funding for the purchase of equipment and materials, but the introduction of LMS and a school policy for the arts offers an opportunity to review the historical model of expenditure. The expressive arts have entered the age of technology and require as basic tools of the trade:

- computers – both for design and for music composition;
- cameras – still and video – and accompanying studio and darkroom equipment;
- recording equipment – both simple and sophisticated;
- musical instruments – traditional and electronic;
- portable lighting bars, etc.

Of course, many of these items have been around for some time and schools have purchased the one-off camera, computer or whatever. What has changed is the scale of the need and the level of dependency upon the new equipment. It is not acceptable to have pupils queueing for long periods of time to use the one computer or the one tape-recorder. The technological explosion offering the right equipment at an affordable price is a fairly recent phenomenon.

The task of changing the perception of senior managers about the expressive arts and their needs may not be easy, but funding for the arts must realistically acknowledge the change of emphasis whilst continuing to provide for a range of media and for a wide variety of supporting resource materials.

Miscellaneous

This catch-all heading is intended here to cover three particular areas of provision which lie less easily elsewhere. These include:

a) *An administration budget*
The demands for copying of various kinds, and for reprographic work in particular, can be considerable in an expressive arts area and may often justify a separate budget heading.

b) *Extra-curricular provision*
As part of an 'arts for all' policy which seeks to provide for each pupil according to his or her level of ability, some extra-curricular activities may legitimately be regarded as an essential extension of the taught provision, and may deserve to be funded as such. In addition, costs associated with exhibitions and displays of work, and with public performances and productions, cannot always be absorbed within the arts budget. Their value as PR investments should be recognised through separate funding.

c) *Enrichment opportunities*
The difficulties generated by the legislation relating to charging for school visits have already been referred to, but they must not be used as an excuse for taking no action. The allocation of some funding for artist residencies, visits, and so on will without doubt attract additional support from other sources such as parents and Regional Arts Associations, if the nature and quality of the work is publicised and the right approaches are made. Because, for some, enrichment opportunities fall into what might be regarded as the discretionary rather than the mandatory category, there is a danger that they can be regarded as an expendable luxury. But if the reader has followed through the argument of the earlier chapters he or she will know that the provision of experience, in addition to the acquisition of skills, is regarded as central to effective arts education. Arts education without enrichment opportunities presents a contradiction in terms.

There will no doubt be other items to enter under the miscellaneous heading, but that option will be left to others.

Organisation

Besides resources, the second significant enabling mechanism is organisation. The major function of organisation is to provide the most effective way of utilising all the resources available – material, physical and, particularly, human – to fulfil the requirements of the aims and the statement of entitlement. A crucial initial policy decision will need to determine the desired level of coordination and coherence between the arts disciplines. It will decide whether the arts will be taught as disparate, discrete disciplines or as a unified and coordinated group of related disciplines. If the latter – which is clearly the view suggested here – then a whole cycle of related issues will require resolution. There will be a need, for example, to consider the correlation and coordination of the individual subject programmes of study to give coherence to an overall development programme, creating in practice a recognisable and comprehensible area of experience. Decisions will need to be made about the use of collaborative or combined projects, and on the uses of time and curriculum organisation which, in turn, will inform timetabling needs. A coherent approach to the curriculum will also underline the need for a shared assessment policy. A possible model has been suggested in chapter 4.

Curriculum organisation of this nature requires a staffing structure and team network which reflect the underlying philosophy. It seems essential for a coordinator to be at the head, but thereafter the shape of the team and the responsibilities of individual members will be determined by local circumstances.

Collectively the points discussed above provide a framework for a school policy for the arts. The diagram on page 154 may provide a helpful summary.

Towards an LEA policy

There are clear parallels between the focal points for a school's arts policy and those for an LEA policy. The differences are primarily concerned with emphasis and scale, the most significant difference being that whilst a school is concerned largely with the educational opportunities of a restricted age range, the LEA has a responsibility for the full age range – from cradle to grave.

The LEA's relationship with the public is, of course, quite different. It lacks the personal contact associated with schooling and, for many, the LEA is synonymous with faceless bureaucracy comprising grey men in grey suits making unimportant decisions. At the same time 'they' – the little grey men from the LEA – will be expected to know the answers and will be expected to provide what no one else will or can provide.

There is more than a grain of truth in this caricature – at least as far as the expectations are concerned! The advisers and officers of the LEA, whilst not occupying high-profile posts, are heavily

TOWARDS A SCHOOL POLICY FOR THE EXPRESSIVE ARTS

```
                                                    Administration
                                                        budget
                                                         |
                                   Modernisation         |
                                    programme            |
                                        |                |
                                        |         MISCELLANEOUS
                                        |         /        \
                                   Technology    /          \
                                        |       /       Extra-curricular
                                        |      /         opportunities
                                   EQUIPMENT/
                                   MATERIALS
                                    /      \
                                   /      Routine    Enrichment
                      Modernisation        costs    opportunities
                       programme
                           |
                           |          Location
                           |         ('faculty/
                      ACCOMMODATION   grouping)
                       /      |
                      /       |
                 Specialist   Quality
                  spaces        of
                     |      environment
                     |
     Nature      STAFFING
       of        /   |   \
    contracts   /    |    \
         |     /     |     \
         |    /      |      \
    Specialisms  Peripatetic  \
                    staff      \
                                Training
        Ratio
                                                 Assessment
                                                   policy
                                                      |
                                                      |
                                  Combined            |
                                  projects            |
                                      \               |
                                       \         COORDINATION
                                        \        /    |
                                         \      /     |
                                          \    /   Timetabling
                                           \  /      needs
                                   Related /
                                 programmes
                                   of study
                                                  Staffing
                                                  structure

  RESOURCING ←———————————————————————————— EVALUATION
       ↑                                        ↑
       |                                        |
       |   STATEMENT OF ENTITLEMENT ————————————┘
       |       FOR ALL PUPILS
       |           ↑
       |           |
  PHILOSOPHY → AIMS ——————→ ORGANISATION
```

154

relied upon for advice, guidance and for all manner of comment and decisions, often leading to far-reaching consequences. The role of the LEA is essentially a supporting and enabling one – frequently supporting in the sense of taking the lead and establishing a path through new and difficult terrain – and that role can be most effectively and satisfactorily fulfilled and understood within the framework of a policy, in this instance an LEA policy for the arts.

Philosophy, understanding and aims

A process similar to that described for schools is appropriate, with homogeneous groups meeting for detailed discussions on specific topics, but with structured overlapping between groups to provide overall coherence. Discussion and debate will need to consider not only the function of the arts in education but also the role of the arts in a wider social context. In the past the track record for effective dialogue between those involved in formal education, adult education, the youth service and various other community groups has not been good, and it can be assumed that, as with the school consultation, there will be a need to clarify terminology, remove misunderstanding and generally share information and perceptions.

Because of the diverse interests represented, it is inevitable and desirable that discussions will range far and wide. It is also true that what individuals can or will wish to take from the discussions will vary enormously. But three goals should be set:

a) to seek agreement on a limited number of aims;

b) to seek a consensus view on the expressive arts in education which all with responsibility for arts disciplines can feel comfortable with;

c) to identify a 'priority' list of needs, to be considered for inclusion in the policy or possibly in a strategy document.

It would be unfortunate if the consultation group evaporated into thin air once the discussions were completed. There is much to commend the stabilising of the group in the form of *an advisory group for the arts*, the function of which would be to provide an interface between the various sectors and thereby to promote/facilitate coherence throughout the education service.

A statement of entitlement

The fact that the clientele is so much wider than the school age range will clearly influence the nature and content of the statement of entitlement. It may be felt, for example, that continuing education catering for the years beyond formal education, could have a compensatory role to perform. As society has moved beyond the manufacturing age, so many have found themselves unemployed for long periods of time whilst others, in employment, find little fulfilment in machine-minding or VDU-gazing. There is more to life than this, and one function of arts education must be to offer opportunity for the acquisition of creative skills which will facilitate the 'reflexive' expression (see Chapter 2) of personal experience.

But there are many routes which lead to this point of need. For some, school days were devoted to the pursuit of skills leading to a 'good job with prospects'. Their education lacked balance in that they closed the door to the expressive disciplines, and only slowly has the missing dimension been identified. Others belatedly discover latent expressive talents; yet others encounter new experiences in life which they cannot explore or communicate for want of an effective expressive vocabulary. And, of course, there are many who will wish to pursue the arts for the intrinsic satisfaction and enjoyment the arts have to offer.

Then, too, there will be an increase in leisure time for most in the future. And the impacts of new technologies on the availability of video, photography, instruments, etc., are irreversible trends of the age.

The statement of entitlement must accommodate all of these situations and more. In essence, the statement should include the opportunity for every citizen, regardless of age, culture, or place of abode, to:

- express, create, and/or perform in any chosen art form;
- enjoy/experience quality through the works of others – e.g. exhibitions, displays, concerts, productions etc;
- receive education in any art form.

Resourcing

With the devolution of spending power to individual schools, the residual LEA purse is obviously considerably reduced. This situation immediately calls for two policy decisions:

a) What services will the LEA continue to provide from the discretionary sum it is allowed to retain?
b) How will the LEA be able to support most effectively existing needs, yet encourage, and no doubt generate, innovation?

The first decision will have important consequences for the future of peripatetic teaching, advisory support services, special project initiatives, resource centres, etc., all of which have in the past contributed significantly to the quality of education and have enhanced the capacity of the education service to initiate and respond to change.

The second decision is multi-faceted and each authority will clearly have its own agenda, but the topics for consideration might well include:

- The ability of the LEA to provide, and perhaps extend, opportunities for excellence. Many authorities currently support music schools and orchestras, dance groups and drama groups – although the visual arts are often neglected. By virtue of the fact that these groups bring together talented pupils from across an LEA, it is not possible for individual schools to offer alternative provision.
- A possible role for the LEA as promoter/broker, engaging artists or companies for residencies and making them available to schools and colleges for an appropriate charge. The advantages to the school are that the pre-selection process should indicate some guarantee of quality, and the block-booking by the LEA should generally reduce costs. For the LEA there is an opportunity to engage exciting and stimulating artists whose influence, it is felt, would be advantageous to the advancement of the arts in the authority. This arrangement would be used to assist, not to replace, the 'matching' process outlined in an earlier chapter. (It may also be easier for the authority to negotiate with the Regional Arts Association and other bodies for additional funding.)
- The provision of a pool of specialist arts teachers whose services can be bought in by schools – either individually, or as a team for a specific project. The value of such a pool to schools lacking specialist expertise could be considerable, and the future demand is unlikely to diminish, particularly for music teachers.
- The central provision of exhibitions and displays which can be hired by establishments to improve the quality of the environment.

Beyond formal schooling there is a need to examine the resource implications of supporting the statement of entitlement in different areas, such as rural communities, the inner cities or other urban developments. In some instances special community projects may be appropriate, and on occasions it could prove cost-effective to subcontract such project work to other agencies. It is also necessary for there to be clear guidelines stating what the LEA can/will support and in what way.

The appointment and training of personnel should figure prominently in the resource agenda. All too often the contracts of animateurs and other arts personnel seem to be dependent upon supplementary short-term funding and they are certainly more vulnerable to the vagaries of LEA budgeting than almost any other category of appointment. There is therefore a need to secure the permanent appointment of animateurs, supported by appropriate training programmes for youth leaders and others, thus establishing a coherent network of provision.

References have been made to the introduction of split contracts in certain circumstances. A contract combining school teaching with work in the community offers one obvious interpretation of this strategy, to the mutual advantage of both sectors. Often officers of the LEA occupy an overview position from which the possibility of such pairings can be identified.

Accommodation

Schools and colleges are expensive plants, sometimes costing more to build, equip and maintain than small industrial concerns. It makes no sense, therefore, that specialist provision should be used on average for no more than five hours per day for forty weeks in the year.

Conversely it makes very good sense to invest more in the schools if, in return, they fulfil more than one function. For example, it would be very feasible to hire out recording facilities or provide gallery accommodation during school holidays. In some instances it may be possible to secure funding from the district council if an additional amenity is being offered to the local community. This arrangement is quite common in relation to sports provision.

Certainly, in the present context, it seems likely that the dual or multiple use of establishments will be explored, and possibly recommendations might be incorporated within the policy for the arts.

Equipment
The arguments associated with the provision of equipment are, in part, an extension of the accommodation issue. Very few LEAs would contemplate setting up video or recording studios purely for community use, and the number of amateur musicians who enjoy the opportunity of using a computer as a facility for composition must be small indeed. And yet the possibilities for such developments exist, or can be encouraged to exist, through shared provision.

For many small schools, particularly primary schools, the loss of a central bank of resources which can be loaned or hired would be disastrous. These schools seldom experience the opportunity to indulge in the 'luxuries' – such as computers, instruments, light bars, stage blocks, recording units, etc. – which larger schools can afford and sometimes take for granted. An LEA resource centre can keep pace with technological developments and can offer advice as well as service. Small schools may also need assistance and/or advice with the maintenance and servicing of equipment already purchased.

Organisation

The above outline provides a wide-ranging survey of areas requiring thought and deliberation during the process leading to the formation of a policy for the arts. Obviously there are others. And yet, important as resources undoubtedly are, it is ultimately people who make things happen and there is no substitute for getting the right people in the right places, and for structuring appropriate channels for communication between them. The art of achieving this is what constitutes good organisation. In the circumstances we are discussing here, organisation will be required to fulfil two functions:

- to provide a coherent structure enabling the aims and the statement of entitlement to be delivered;
- to carry out the effective management of the resources provided for that purpose.

The greatest impediments to the creation and implementation of a coordinated policy for the arts are likely to be historic patterns of organisation, and the associated habits and ways of thinking. It may be helpful to refer briefly to what needs to be achieved:
a) There must be a match between the stated philosophy of the

LEA and the way in which the education department is seen to be organised. If the philosophy advocates collaboration between the arts in schools and yet the LEA continues to organise itself on a discrete arts basis, possibly with the advisory support groups for the various disciplines located at different centres, then the messages going out to schools are both contradictory and confusing.

b) There must be some provision made for continued consultation following the formation of the policy. If participants are allowed to return to their separate departments and activities with no network in place to facilitate further involvement, the process will be perceived to have been a shallow paper exercise of little durable value. The formation of *an advisory group for the arts*, mentioned above, offers one possible response.

c) There is a need to overcome the 'strata vision' of education – the notion that the pupil proceeds from the primary layer to the secondary layer and then breaks the surface into the great unknown. Fortunately changes in education generally are accelerating the demise of this model. The National Curriculum is demanding knowledge and understanding of the mechanisms and structures of the world beyond school, and the need for continuity between phases is inculcating the habit of meaningful liaison between groups and institutions.

Personal growth and need in the expressive arts seldom follow a linear pattern of development, and certainly not a pattern that can be closely aligned with chronological age. Adults frequently need an opportunity to use equipment, or to re-explore techniques they left behind in the second 'layer': some pupils would benefit enormously (and in some instances do) from the challenge of interactions which fall outside the restrictive schedule of the school curriculum. The fact is that arts experience, and the urge to be creative, cannot be contained in tight time capsules labelled 'age 10', 'age 15', 'classical', 'pop', etc., and there is often a conflict between the *real* needs of the individual and the *perceived* needs as decreed by history, tradition and administrative convenience.

This is not an invitation to anarchy. It is a suggestion that the type of consultation process advocated here could contribute significantly to an increased awareness of opportunities, needs and problems and could consider possible lines of development. There are many community schools throughout the country with useful experience to offer.

Central Government and an arts education policy

To outline a national policy would be both self-indulgent and a waste of time. But it is not unreasonable to use the opportunity to identify a limited number of areas in which comparatively modest adjustments within the existing framework could greatly assist the cause of arts education:

a) *The equal status of arts subjects within the National Curriculum*
However unnecessary it may appear to the politician or the layperson, there really is a need to give all expressive arts disciplines clearly recognisable equality of status, thus avoiding the present nonsensical hierarchical discrimination. There is no sound educational argument against such a move, and political resistance may have ebbed with the tide.

There are those – including some headteachers and governors – who, by inclination or through lack of time, read only the 'headlines' or digests and attach little importance to all else. When this superficial approach is reflected in the appointment of staff and the allocation of resources, serious curriculum black holes can develop.

The interrelationship between the expressive arts disciplines should also be recognised and reinforced in the organisational structures of the DES, the NCC and SEAC.

b) *Grant targeting*
Fine words of reassurance from education ministers regarding the importance of the arts in education are very welcome but such statements would gain credibility, and the status of the arts would be greatly enhanced, if words were accorded financial support. The need is clear. The inadequacy in training for arts teachers is now well documented, and the HMI report 'Standards in Education 1987–88' commented that in secondary schools music and the other arts subjects are *'still under-valued and under-provided for, and pupils' aesthetic responses and creative experiences are relatively poorly developed'*. Throughout the entire development of the grant-targeting process in recent years, and the accumulated extensive list of priority headings, I can recall no reference to the expressive arts at national level – although many LEAs have promoted local initiatives.

There is an urgent need to respond to the unsatisfactory situations referred to above, and also to enrich such areas as special needs, and youth and adult education.

c) *The Education Reform Act and charging for out-of-school activities*
That part of the Act relating to charges for school visits and such activities as instrumental tuition has clearly produced 'unfortunate' consequences, most of which should have been anticipated. The situation is likely to be aggravated as the Local Management of Schools legislation is implemented. Any form of provision which depends upon voluntary contributions from parents must inevitably result in inequality between one area and another, and between one school and another. If one adds to this the wide-ranging differences in attitude towards peripatetic instrumental tuition, the inequality becomes even more pronounced. Such extremes are not acceptable within a *state* education system.

Some teachers are confused, some are inhibited, and some are intimidated by the legislation. Certainly it displays little understanding of life in the classroom where the hassle of chasing up voluntary contributions from recalcitrant parents (who 'know their rights') is an unnecessary, externally generated pressure. Until all contributions have been received, pre-booking can be a precarious business. It is not surprising that galleries, museums, companies providing schools matinées, heritage properties, etc., all report drastic reductions in attendance figures. Most importantly the legislation is inadvertently impeding experiential learning and direct access to the arts experience.

d) *Accessibility to the arts*
The theme of accessibility to the arts is worth pursuing. In any form of communication, lack of familiarity with the medium obviously causes unintelligibility. This is glaringly apparent in the case of communication through a foreign language but is equally true of communication through the expressive arts. In the latter instance, this lack of familiarity sometimes mistakenly leads to the description of an art form as élitist, the implication being that it can only be understood or enjoyed by a small minority. The fact is that, given the opportunity, the art form can be understood by most but circumstances such as cost prevent it from becoming a regular and familiar experience. For example, there is abundant evidence to demonstrate that pupils of all ages and levels of ability are able to enjoy both opera and ballet, always assuming, of course, that an appropriate choice of work has been made and that the necessary preparation has been undertaken. It is not an introduction to these art forms which presents a problem but rather the ability to provide a regularity of encounter sufficient

to generate confidence and broaden understanding of the conventions and vocabularies of the respective art forms. Currently there is little chance of sustaining interest created through schools matinée performances when the costs for public performances are prohibitive. This absence of opportunity is exacerbated for those who live in the provinces and are dependent on touring companies. Opera, particularly, is an extremely expensive art form which, as a general rule, needs to be performed in a confined space, thereby restricting the size of audience and consequently increasing the price of admission. Although recent surveys have shown the considerable, and growing, popularity of the art form, it will never be possible to produce opera performances of high quality which are self-supporting without charging prices which make them inaccessible to the vast majority of the population – thus perpetuating the élitist image.

For its part, Central Government could readily improve pupil accessibility to the arts by:

- monitoring more closely the nature and effectiveness of education programmes undertaken by major companies in receipt of Arts Council subsidy and, where appropriate, by rewarding progressive companies in order that their education work might be extended;
- encouraging companies generally (if necessary through financial inducement) to explore ways of sustaining pupils' contacts through appropriate programme choice, preferential concessionary booking (packaged to facilitate regular attendance over an extended period), and other similar initiatives;
- increasing the level of support to touring companies or, preferably, by encouraging the creation of a limited number of permanent companies outside London. Can it be that after 1992 Britain's attitude towards public subsidy for the arts will be influenced by our neighbours on the Continent?

e) *Grants for arts development*
Specialist facilities and equipment for joint use, discussed earlier in this chapter, are expensive to provide, but the burden can be eased if the cost is shared between a number of interested parties. A model for such a partnership has existed for some years in the world of sport, where the Sports Council has contributed significantly to collaborative development programmes serving areas and communities. Unfortunately the Arts Council has no similar

remit. There are many reasons why this situation should be reviewed, among which the greater availability of free time in which people can be actively creative is perhaps the most important.

Politicians who in the past have been hesitant to declare their support for the arts should think again. The Policy Studies Institute report provided firm evidence that the common view of the arts as a minority interest is misleading. In fact, the arts reach two-thirds of the population. The Institute's research also found that 51% of the public was in favour of maintaining the level of government support, 35% thought it should be increased, while only 4% thought it should be decreased, and 2% thought it should be stopped.

There is clearly scope and public support for development in the arts. As a nation we sell ourselves short if we neglect to invest in the aesthetic, the creative and the expressive. The indications are that we instinctively, if coyly, recognise the fact. The true quality of life (Witkin's *'world within oneself'*) is ill-served by political philosophies which marginalise the arts. We have an obligation to communicate our wishes to our elected representatives who, in turn, have a responsibility to respond positively to the will of the people. If we fail to make the case known, the loss is ours as a society.

CHAPTER 9 EFFECTING CHANGE

People and change

Change in education is concerned with people. Resistance to change in education is also concerned with people: their vanities and their fears. The two qualities are often so inextricably interwoven that it is difficult to distinguish one from the other. The vanity which thirsts for recognition, flattery, reward and status is easily bruised and is highly vulnerable to change – and there is some streak of that vanity in most of us. It has access to considerable reserves of emotional energy which can be used either positively or negatively. Vanity is precious, and is for ever on its guard, hence the close association with fear.

The essence of fear is uncertainty. In most areas of human activity it is possible to come to terms with the known, even in extremely difficult circumstances, but the unknown (uncertainty) constantly nags and is capable of evoking stress, uncharacteristic behaviour and passionate outbursts from otherwise placid and balanced individuals.

In terms of curriculum or organisational change there are two frequent areas of contention created by uncertainty. The first is the threat to security a teacher can experience when the status quo is threatened. This may be in the form of a proposed change to a routine, or a syllabus amendment which perhaps disturbs a teaching pattern established over a long period, or a required adjustment of teaching style. Teaching is a profession in which confidence is a key requisite and it is not difficult to appreciate that any change which, even temporarily, might shake that confidence can be seen as a threat. For most the familiar is comfortable, and there are many who dislike having to think again. Innovation = new = disturbance and the need to break established habits and patterns in favour of new ones, possibly without being sure initially of what the new requirements are or will be. Therefore (the argument continues) innovation should be treated with suspicion – particularly if, in addition, it involves changed relationships, including, perhaps, working with teachers from other disciplines for the first time.

The second area of difficulty concerns the perceived threat to the status of a particular discipline, and all that that implies. There are examples in many of our schools where a teacher has spent much of his or her teaching career nurturing and establishing a particular subject or discipline. As the subject has grown, so has the teacher's own status within the school, perhaps acknowledged by the awarding of a responsibility allowance. Proposed changes may require that discipline to become part of a larger department – in this case an expressive arts 'faculty' – with the teacher losing some of the autonomy so hard-earned over a number of years, and possibly with a reduced allocation of teaching time as all pupils are offered a broadly based arts education. Only the totally insensitive could fail to appreciate the feelings that teacher would be likely to experience during a prolonged period of uncertainty. Only the callous would fail to take measures or adopt strategies to reduce that uncertainty. In such circumstances the irony is that it is often the teacher's own single-mindedness and dedication which have blinkered him or her from the changes occurring in the world outside – changes which can no longer be ignored.

More recently a third, subsidiary fear has begun to surface with some degree of regularity: the fear or suspicion (the more cynical face of uncertainty) that change will involve an increased amount of paperwork. Such an attitude is understandable in the light of the considerable demands which are now made upon the teacher – coursework assesments, Records of Achievement, profiling, etc. – compared with a few years ago, and the full impact of the 1988 Act will clearly further increase rather than decrease the load.

But, of course, many teachers and administrators relish change. Just as there are those who immediately erect the barriers at the first suggestion of change, there are others who become excited and energised by the challenge of something new. The reasons for the contrasting responses are numerous and very varied – perhaps partly due to natural temperament; the general mood and appetite for innovation generated within a particular school or department; the amount 'at stake' – the level of 'vested interest'; and so on. Whatever the pattern of responses may be, the important fact is that the teachers provide the raw material from which curriculum change is built and the sensible builder will study his or her materials very carefully before starting work. There is an often repeated truism, *'you don't change the curriculum – you change people'*, which should be writ large in the office or study of everyone involved in educational management. One of the arts of managing educational change rests in allowing enough time for the people to change without losing the momentum generated by the initial cause. Being sensitive to, and aware of, the reactions of the people who will be most directly affected must not inhibit change, but it should certainly influence the chosen strategy and plan of action.

Why change?

The reasons for change range from the flippant and irritating to the rational and irresistible. Change purely for the sake of change is seldom a good thing – although what appears superficially to be an unecessary change is often a ploy for reactiviting a fossilised area of the curriculum. There are 'anticipated' periods of change which are part of educational culture, such as the changes associated with the arrival of a new, key member of staff. This may be a headteacher, a deputy head with curriculum responsibilities, a head of department or an assistant teacher with some particular area of specialism. Then, of course, there is also 'unavoidable' change inflicted from without, perhaps as a result of school reorganisation or amalgamation.

The notion of the 'unavoidable' or the 'inevitable' is an important concept to grasp during the implementation of change. The feeling that a decision is a *fait accompli* and that change is being belligerently imposed provides a rallying point for unified resistance, at least temporarily. Where the imposition ensues from the Department of Education and Science or from the National Curriculum Council, the problem is a national one and is not perceived as a personal rebuff. An LEA decision may be regarded more seriously and opposed more vehemently. Where the imposition is localised within a particular school context the problem takes on a new dimension. If, in this case, the resistance is total, it suggests either that the reasons are not valid and need to be re-examined, that they have been badly presented, or that insufficient groundwork has been done to prepare staff for the possibility of change – that is, there has been insufficient time or opportunity for the people to begin to change.

The psychology of change demonstrates repeatedly that change cannot be successfully foisted on people from the outside. Only structure can be imposed, not belief. The more vigorously change is pursued, the deeper the resistance will become. The individual feels cornered, with escape routes cut off, and may reach the point where the ego is threatened. Such a mood of conflict is counter-productive since ultimate success will depend upon growing cooperation rather than permanent simmering opposition.

The reasons for change must therefore be sound and convincing – perhaps emerging naturally from a curriculum review. Teachers will quite properly be seeking answers to two questions:

- In what ways are the changes expected to produce an improvement?
- How will they affect me?

(No doubt some teachers will wish to ask these questions in reverse order!)

The extent to which these two questions can be satisfactorily answered will determine the momentum with which change can be implemented. The ideal combination of factors leading to change would comprise sound educational reasoning (i.e. the search for a balanced arts provision within a balanced whole curriculum) associated with good existing practice provided by able, enthusiastic and knowledgeable teachers who could participate constructively in the consultation process. At the other end of the continuum, the school which has no developed philosophy for the arts and inadequate teachers who, for whatever reasons, have no appetite for change, clearly has a problem. It also has the greatest need for change! Most schools will, of course, be somewhere between these two extremes.

Consultation

Theoreticians (and teachers' unions) tell us that if the people to be affected by change are fully consulted from the outset, many of the potential problems will simply not materialise. In practice it is not so easy. Change is often necessary precisely because the existing head of department, or perhaps a whole department, has failed to recognise the need to modify the system of organisation, the syllabus content or the teaching styles. On occasions there is a willingness to change, but a failure to see how change can be implemented, and possibly (in the expressive arts area) a total lack of understanding of such concepts as combined arts or multi-discipline projects. In such circumstances consultation is scarcely an apt definition of the process which must take place. The first stage requires the careful education of the teachers to ensure that there is a thorough grasp of what is being discussed. Only then are the teachers able to contribute usefully. The nature, scope and frequency of consultation will therefore be determined by the state of readiness of the teachers to be involved. Each headteacher tends to cultivate a personal style of consultation which then permeates the working of the whole school, but there are certain skeletal characteristics which most successful managers of change seem to share. These are:

a) *Consultation without handing over the initiative to others*
In full staff meetings or departmental meetings, the manager will listen carefully to what is said, and will demonstrate that he or she has listened by referring regularly to comments made or arguments advanced. But such occasions will be used as opportunities for information gathering and exchange, and not for decision-making. Any form of vote-taking will generally be avoided. Consultation is about taking counsel. It is about inviting and listening to the views of others.

b) *Precise focusing on items for consideration*
The effective agenda addresses one item or theme at a time and, when concerned with change, generally sequences those items to progress from the less contentious to the potentially more contentious areas. The advantages of this process are:

- it provides an early opportunity to establish firmly the common ground and to generate an atmosphere of mutual respect based on broad agreement;
- it simultaneously indicates to the perceptive manager how much 'education' is necessary before it is wise to proceed from one item to the next, and thereby influences the pace of events;
- it 'draws the sting' of protesters hell-bent on blanket criticism if they are first invited to agree on some issues, and their voices are then heard on other specific items as and when they occur on the agenda.

c) *Timing*
A sense of timing is perhaps the greatest gift any manager could wish for! Often success or failure is determined more by timing than by the quality of the decisions taken – and the successful

manager of change has an instinct for timing. The time factor is crucial to several of the points discussed so far – the period of uncertainty; time for people to change; the state of readiness of the teachers; the pace of events. Much, of course, depends on whether change is possible by evolution rather than by revolution, and that decision will reflect the ethos of the individual school. But in general the three guiding principles relating to timing are:

- Avoid shock. Shock produced by the sudden unexpected announcement of change often evokes fear and negative responses. It can be reduced or avoided either through consultation and discussion, or by signalling that some form of change may be necessary.
- Reduce the period of uncertainty to the minimum through dialogue, consultation and an adequate supply of information.
- Allow time for people to change – time for new ideas to be reflected upon and absorbed – and provide support for that time to be used effectively through 'education', consultation, etc.

d) *Encouragement of participation by all*
The most useful and constructive ideas seldom come from the most vociferous staff, and certainly there is no monopoly of good ideas – not even with the headteacher! Often a quiet teacher, or a junior member of staff, has a significant contribution to make but may feel intimidated by the atmosphere of a full staff meeting. The effective manager will devise strategies which enable to voices of all to be heard. One method is to invite written comments or responses. This method has two particular advantages in that it enables the contributor to be more thorough and expansive than is possible in a meeting situation, and it affords the manager the opportunity to refer to the response as often as he or she chooses. An alternative method is to arrange (quite informally) a series of one-to-one chats which enable the manager to pick up and pursue useful suggestions, whilst also offering the opportunity to allay fears and dispel misconceptions. The one-to-one dialogue formula also provides the network through which the manager can focus on those key individual teachers who often influence the judgements made by their colleagues.

Collecting information one way or another supplies the manager with much useful material, both in terms of ideas and staff reactions. It also reassures teachers to know that their voices have been heard. The strategy allows the manager to make whatever decision he or she wishes, providing the message is clearly conveyed that in making the decision full consideration has been given to the range of advice and opinions received. The aim is to provide a framework for action which displays clarity of purpose and, hopefully, some degree of shared ownership. The extent to which this aim is achieved will determine the enthusiasm with which the programme for change is undertaken.

Decision-making is the responsibility of the manager – whether the manager is a headteacher, deputy head or head of department. Once the decision to proceed has been taken, the subject should no longer be open to debate, although the question of *how* to proceed may well require further discussion.

Towards implementation

It can be assumed that the consultative process will have considered in some depth the anticipated benefits of the proposed changes and will have discussed the expected and desired outcomes, certainly in so far as they affect the teachers. The 'How will the changes affect me?' question posed earlier provides the key to a smooth or rough transition period, depending on the response. The teacher will be looking for job and role clarification within any revised structure, and will doubtless be scrutinizing new departmental relationships and relative status, for status is a hard-earned and treasured possession. What will be the working conditions? What will be the degree of autonomy? (For some have much to lose, as was illustrated earlier.) What will be the prospects for professional development? There will also be questions to answer regarding possible adjustments to the teaching programme, the nature of the workload, and changes of teaching style. Collectively such queries, doubts and fears threaten the security of the teacher and may seriously undermine self-confidence and morale. They cannot be dismissed as trivial.

(It is an important lesson in management to realise that attention to seemingly small personal matters is often a far more effective way of 'making things happen' than weighty argument and rhetoric. To remember that a teacher's spouse or child has not been well and to display a genuine interest in their health can promote an amazing degree of cooperation in response. This is not to advocate devious strategies as a means of getting one's own way, it is quite simply to observe that people in high places making momentous decisions are inclined to overlook the bread-and-butter priorities of their 'subordinates'. Their perspectives are different, and until the manager can view the world through the other person's eyes success, in terms of the manager's ability to motivate that person, will be limited.)

The teacher will also be looking for signs of the school's genuine commitment to the process of change. All too often teachers have been required to implement change without adequate resourcing. During a period when changes have been introduced one after another with indecent haste, many teachers feel that they have reached saturation point and expect any further changes to be fully resourced not only with human and physical resources but also, when necessary, with an appropriate allocation of non-contact time in which to undertake essential administration and planning.

Similarly there is a need for the school to demonstrate its commitment through the provision of a staff development training programme. The main aim of such a programme should be to generate confidence and to reassure teachers that they have the skills or the potential to meet the new demands. In order to fulfil this aim the training programme will need to begin *before* the planned change is implemented, but must also continue into the period of change, to address issues and provide support as the need arises.

The training must be available at all levels. The new 'coordinator', for instance, will be entering unfamiliar territory. A matching between the job description and the coordinator's previous experience will obviously identify an initial list of training needs, but a programme based on this list alone might ensure competence rather than stimulate flair. The coordinator will have new ideas, and will require more new ideas. He or she will also benefit considerably from the opportunity to see how colleagues in similar posts of responsibility have coped in other establishments. Any training programme should therefore provide contact with 'new' thinking and with varied examples of good practice. Ultimately the coordinator will have acquired an extensive bank of ideas and knowledge, underpinned by the excitement generated by being newly appointed, and by experience – both personal, and second-hand as recounted by others during school visits.

Depending on the coordinator's personal previous experience, there may also be a need for training in interpersonal skills and management styles. Since the role is so crucial to the successful implementation of change, it makes good sense for the school to invest generously in the coordinator's training.

At assistant teacher level, the most conspicuous need is to provide a training programme which breaks down the barriers between the disciplines and which contributes positively to team-building. Whilst in some instances the barriers are very real and have been created to protect 'subject territory', there are many cases where divisions occur through ignorance rather than through wilful exclusion. The problem belongs essentially to the secondary phase where very few arts specialists have a working knowledge in an expressive arts discipline other than their own. Increasingly secondary teachers are asking for opportunities to experience other disciplines, and they enjoy participating in combined arts in-service courses which positively encourage such a change of activity. However brief the encounter with the non-specialist art form may be, it will no doubt focus the awareness and add meaning to further 'departmental' discussions between arts teachers. Such enrichment opportunities can contribute significantly to the successful unifying of a newly formed expressive arts group.

Team-building can be encouraged through sessions in which the teachers share a common objective, such as exploring the commonalities in terminology and concepts which occur across the expressive arts disciplines, or in working together to create the framework for a combined arts project. The exchanges and discussions which are integral to such meetings should greatly enhance understanding whilst promoting collaboration. Then, too, there will need to be an agreed and shared policy on assessment, recording and reporting. Again the necessary debate should encourage cohesion within the group. As with the co-ordinator's training, so the assistant teachers will benefit from visiting other schools to experience examples of good practice. This is particularly important to the uncommited or sceptical teacher. Such visits provide the most effective response to the 'It can't be done' attitude.

In all training sessions it is important to guarantee the high quality of the provider. A major function of the leader of any training session is to enthuse, to excite, and to stimulate as well as to inform. Often the school can be dependent upon the training provider for motivation. A mistake can prove costly, for a 'disastrous' session can be a waste of money, a waste of time and, most important, may discourage teachers from further involvement in any similar activity. Key catalysts for change can be the Advisory Teachers. They possess the skills, have the necessary range of contacts to locate for dissemination examples of good practice, and they work with individual schools in the school's own isolated context, examining the questions/problems pertinent to that particular situation. Good Advisory Teachers also have credibility and are respected and trusted by teacher colleagues.

Change is an organic process and the maturation period can be long, yet frequently the instigator of change wants immediate results. Therein exists a tension, and the inexperienced innovator may well become frustrated by delays and may attempt to short-circuit the process. Such impatience seldom saves time in the long term. In the expressive arts a typical example might be the school which devises an arts policy requiring *all* pupils to be taught *all* arts disciplines to the age of 14. This policy, it is decided, will be fully implemented from the following September. Whilst the policy in itself is perfectly admirable, if the full implementation in September means that boys of 13+ suddenly find themselves in dance lessons, having had no previous involvement in the discipline, then the school is clearly inviting trouble! It would require an extremely charismatic teacher in a fully supportive environment to translate successfully the well-intentioned but mistaken decision into practice. The likelihood is that such a move would be less than wholly successful and that the decision would have to be reviewed. Once dance had become established in the curriculum for 11 and 12-year-olds, then would be the time to consider the full implementation of the policy. Because growth is organic, there will be little blossom and no fruit until the roots have well and truly taken and have been nurtured with adequate resources and appropriate training for the teachers.

The cell by cell approach is also necessary where the general climate remains lukewarm and unenthusiastic. In such circumstances no amount of debate and discussion is likely to change the situation. The most effective way forward is by example. This may initially involve just two or three teachers collaborating within a comparatively restricted area. In the early stages this matters not: the quality of the work produced, together with the level of enthusiasm and motivation generated, is more important than the immediate range of influence. From such a caucus, further developments will inevitably follow.

Change from below

The discussion to this point has been concerned primarily with change initiated from above, from management level, but of course there is no reason why the impetus for change should not originate at any level. It remains true, however, that instigating change from assistant teacher level is not easy in most schools, and we have already commented on the teacher who returns from an in-service course full of enthusiasm and energy only to be frustrated by a lack of interest from senior staff, or by a pervasive atmosphere of doom and gloom. At such a time the assistant teacher becomes extremely conscious of his or her lack of status and lack of power. There is a recognition of dependency on the decisions and whims of others, who all too frequently seem to be obdurate and lacking in vision.

Above all, the assistant teacher who wishes to initiate change will need to possess the qualities of patience and humility. Patience is necessary for two associated reasons. First, the lack of a power base means that the teacher has little control over the speed of change, which in turn means that progress is almost invariably slower than the teacher would wish – sometimes very much slower! Second, managers as well as assistant staff need time to acclimatise to the possibility of change, and there may be a prolonged period of drip-feeding ideas and information in preparation for persuading the head, or whoever, to make the 'right' decision. Humility is necessary because, sadly, the best ideas are often appropriated by managers and presented as their own, without acknowledgement to the source of origin! This is good in so far as it accelerates change, but is very damaging to the ego.

So what strategies might the assistant teacher adopt in order to introduce a new idea in an establishment which is heavily sceptical of anything innovative? I suggest there are three approaches which can be used independently or collectively according to circumstances. They are:

a) *Achieving change by example*

The purpose of this approach is obviously to reassure, or silence, the doubters. There are occasions when change is resisted because others do not fully comprehend what is being suggested, or because they fail to appreciate the full implications of what is being proposed. In such cases the status quo is often the preferred option. On other occasions resistance emanates from the 'It can't be done!' fraternity. In either case, the best answer is clearly to demonstrate that it can be done and simultaneously to provide evidence of the advantages gained.

The teacher may be working alone, depending on the particular situation, but if possible it is helpful to seek out a kindred spirit or spirits and to operate as a small group. Care should be taken not to flaunt what is being done in an 'I told you so' manner, but rather work should be undertaken discreetly and unostentatiously but with regular memos being sent to key personnel to acquaint them with progress. Such memos also form part of the drip-feed strategy referred to above which introduces others to the need for, or possibility of, change. If the 'pilot project' is successful it will no doubt generate interest and may well attract a degree of support which would make its rejection difficult.

b) *Finding the lever of change*

Every organisation has both a formal and an informal network of 'command'. That is to say that outside the formal hierarchy there are people whose opinions are counselled and valued more highly than others and who exercise a degree of influence when decisions are made. Schools present no exception to the general rule and, indeed, there can be few organisations where the informal network is more rife than in a school staffroom. The 'aware' teacher will not seek to impress all and sundry with the immense benefits of the new idea, but will be selective and will carefully observe *who* needs to be persuaded.

c) Don't go to the head with a problem – unless you also have a solution! Perhaps the most characteristic feature of headship is the diversity of problems which somehow become the head's 'lot'. Earlier in this chapter the point was made that it is necessary for any successful manager to appreciate the bread-and-butter concerns of his or her employees. In a similar way it is important for the employee to realise that the manager's, the head's, problems extend far beyond the needs of any one curriculum area. It follows that the amount of focused time which can be devoted solely to any one area will be small indeed. Hence the injunction at the beginning of the paragraph. The fact is that pressures on the head's time can be used to the teacher's advantage.

Some years ago I was advised by an experienced deputy head on the strategy for getting a head's approval for a proposed scheme. His technique was that, on entering the head's room, the teacher would suggest that there was a problem, and would then proceed to outline the magnitude, possible consequences and implications of a deteriorating situation. The teacher would watch carefully as the head sank lower and lower in his or her seat and then, at the opportune moment, would interject 'But I think I have a solution'. The head, with an abundance of other problems to resolve, would happily grasp at the straw so generously offered. A decision would be reached and a crisis averted to the satisfaction of all.

I have subsequently operated at both ends of this strategy and know that it works! Heads seldom have time or opportunity to give sustained thought to one particular problem, and any teacher who *thoroughly* plans a case and takes care with its presentation must stand a reasonable chance of obtaining approval for its implementation. Whilst the technique, as outlined, may smack of cynicism, the principle is absolutely valid and should be taken to heart. Heads do not enjoy being left with problems. They are much happier approving solutions!

In conclusion

The central theme of this chapter has been that to understand change, to effect change successfully, demands first an understanding of human nature and then, more specifically, an understanding of, and consideration for, the individuals who will be involved in the process. Change is seldom easily achieved, regardless of the justification for its introduction. It was ever thus. Four centuries ago Richard Hooker wrote: '*Change is not made without inconvenience, even from worse to better*'. But I would wish to conclude where I began, and remind the reader that one of the aims identified in the Introduction was: '*To advocate a strong contempt for the impossible and a determination to take full advantage of the opportunities presented within a changing scene*'.

For all involved in expressive arts education the next few years will be of vital importance. We cannot shirk the challenge they offer. We cannot ignore the opportunity for beneficial change. My hope is that some of the thoughts expressed in these pages may contribute to that process of change.

BIBLIOGRAPHY

Abbs, P. (1982), *English Within the Arts* (Hodder and Stoughton)
Abbs, P. (1975), *Reclamations: Essays on Culture, Mass Culture and the Curriculum* (Gryphon Press)
Assessment of Performance Unit (1983), 'Aesthetic Development' (APU)
Best, D. (1985), *Feeling and Reason in the Arts* (Allen and Unwin)
Black, P. (1987), 'Task Group on Assessment and Testing Report' (DES)
DES (1985), 'Better Schools' (DES)
Dyson, A. (1983), 'Preface' in *Art Education: Heritage and Prospect* (ed Dyson) (University of London Institute of Education)
'Education Reform Act' 1988
Eisner, E. W. (1985), *The Art of Educational Evaluation* (Falmer Press)
Gibson, R. (1983), *The Education of Feeling* (Cambridge Institute of Education)
Green Paper (1977), 'Education in Our Schools' (HMSO)
Gulbenkian Foundation (1982), 'The Arts in Schools' (Gulbenkian Foundation)
Heyfron, V. (1986) 'Objectivity and Assessment in Art' in *Assessment in Arts Education* (ed Ross) (Pergamon)
HMI Series; Curriculum Matters 2 (1985), 'The Curriculum from 5 to 16' (HMSO)
HMI (1977), 'Curriculum 11–16' (DES)
HMI (1987), 'Quality in Schools: The Initial Training of Teachers' (HMSO)
HMI (1989), 'Standards in Education 1987–88' (DES)
Hudson, L. (1966) *Contrary Imaginations* (Penguin)
Natonal Curriculum Council (1988), 'A Framework for the Primary Curriculum' (NCC)
National Foundation for Education Research (1986), 'The Arts: A Preparation to Teach' (A Study of Initial Training for Primary Teachers) (NFER)
Paine, S. (1983) 'Progress and Paradox in Drawing' in *Art*

Education: Heritage and Prospect (ed Dyson) (University of London Institute of Education)
Policy Studies Institute (1989), *The Economic Importance of the Arts in Britain* (PSI)
Reid, L. A. (1980), 'Meaning in the Arts' in *The Arts and Personal Growth* (ed Ross) (Pergamon)
Reid, L. A. (1986), *Ways of Understanding and Education* (Heinemann Educational Books)
Ross, M. (1975), *Arts and the Adolescent* (Schools Council, Evans)
Ross, M. (1984), *The Aesthetic Impulse* (Pergamon)
Ross, M. (1989), 'The Arts in the Primary School: Reforming Teacher Education' (Gulbenkian Foundation)
Witkin, R. (1974) *The Intelligence of Feeling* (Heinemann Educational Books)

INDEX

accommodation 150–1, 158
accountability and educational practice 15–16
administration budget 152
adolescence 37, 65
advisory teachers 124, 174
aesthetic awareness 31, 32, 60
appraisal 103–4 (*see also* assessment and evaluation)
artists' residencies
　extended 143
　funding and organising 137–9, 152
　planning 132–7
　single-session 142
　sources of artists 134–7
　value of 121, 128–32
arts
　analysis of importance 18–19, 25–8, 40–1
　defined 7
　and the economy 41
　historic status within curriculum 12–13
　present status within curriculum 9, 20, 96
Arts Council of Great Britain (ACGB) 137
arts education
　concerns of 7, 23, 31, 146–7
　differing interpretations 13–14
arts experience 7–8
arts policy (LEA)
　consultative basis 155, 160
　implementation 159–60
　policy areas 156–9
　statement of entitlement 156
arts policy (school)
　consultative basis 145–6
　foundation 145
　need for 24, 144–5
　policy areas 148–53
　statement of entitlement 147–8
arts weeks 74–6
assessment and evaluation
　need for 91–2
　ongoing process 42–3
　perceptions of 92–3, 94–7
　profile 56–7, 101–4
　techniques 111–12
　tools and models 20
assistant teachers 173, 175
attainment targets 71, 77, 93, 95
aural literacy 38–9
awareness 31, 33, 35

balance within curriculum 62–3
breadth of experience 63–4
British Film Institute (BFI) 137

Callaghan, James, Ruskin College speech (1976) 15
Central Government
　and accessibility to the arts 161–3
　grant targeting 161
　and National Curriculum 161
change
　achieving by example 175–6
　with consultation 168–71
　impetus from below 175–7
　implementation 171–7
　reasons for 167–8
　resistance to 165–7
　towards child-centred education 14–15
child-centred education, movement towards 14–15
collaboration
　benefits 19
　between disciplines 72–3, 113, 173
　between schools 105–6, 114, 126
combined arts approach *see* collaboration, between disciplines
community dimension to arts education 23, 158
comparison of work 98
completion of work 55–6
comprehensive school system 14, 17
computer technology 110–11

181

constructive comment 57, 98
continuous time pattern 73–4
coordinators 21, 82, 83, 172–3
creative capacity 30–1
creative process
  phases 30–1, 42–58
  skills and attitudes involved 29–30
critical faculty, developing 104
critical studies 57
criticism 97, 98
cultural environment 38
'Curriculum 11–16' ('Red Book') 16, 20, 59
curriculum
  'assembly' and 'design' models 109
  characteristics 62–6
  funding 83
  modular 74
  organisation 152–3
  and targeted funding 17
curriculum development
  aims 60–1
  determining content 66–71
  emergence of concept 15
  GCSE requirements 111–12
  influence of 'Curriculum 11–16' 16
curriculum of entitlement 59, 147
curriculum leaders 124
curriculum statements 60

dance 77, 100, 122–3
demotivators 97–8
departmental restructuring 113–14
descriptive vocabulary 45
design and fine art polarisation 77
development plans 23, 24, 83, 84
devolved funding 91
differentiation 64–5, 68
drama 100, 122–3

economy, national, the arts within 41
'Education in Schools: A Consultative Document' (1977) 15
education of the senses and emotions 26, 34–7
educational function of the arts 7
effective teaching 106–7
efficient teaching 106, 107
11+ examination 12
élitist image of art 162–3
emotional response 33, 35, 36, 37
emotional vocabulary 34–5
enrichment opportunities 147, 152

environment, quality of 80, 151
equipment and materials 62–3, 151, 159
exchange of teachers 121
exhibition of work 81
experiential learning 25, 27, 35
extended courses 120, 123
extended time pattern 74–6
extra-curricular provision 23, 79–80, 152, 161–2

film-making 38
flexibility 72, 113
freedom of expression 14
funding
  devolved 91
  residencies 137–8
  resources 148
  targeted 17–18

General Certificate of Secondary Education (GCSE) 18, 19, 111
gestation of ideas 53–4
good practice, dissemination of 123, 173
governing bodies
  and an arts policy 146
  and Local Management of Schools 21–2
grading 99
grammar schools 12–13
Grant Related In-Service Training System (GRIST) 17–18, 20, 119
grant targeting 161
grants for arts development 163–4
growth phase of creative process 54–5
Gulbenkian Report 13, 20, 41, 96, 150

headteachers 21, 117, 176–7
hidden curriculum 80–1

image vocabulary 28
in-service training 20, 24, 113, 114, 119, 149–50, 172
inhibitors of creative abilities 28–9
inspiration *see* stimulus
integrated curriculum 77–9
integrated teaching approach 19, 83
interrupted time pattern 74

job sharing 126

knowledge, assessing 102

Local Education Authority (LEA)
  Advisory Services 134
  and collaboration arrangements 126
  financial control 21
  provision of services and
    opportunities 157-9
  role in training 122-4
Local Education Authority
  Training Grants Scheme (LEATGS)
  119, 120
Local Management of Schools (LMS)
  21-3, 91, 113, 126, 144-5
long-term planning 122

management training 116-17
medium
  conventions of 44
  exploration of 43, 44, 62
  vocabulary 43-4
modular curriculum 74
motivation 57, 98-9
multicultural teaching 63-4
music 12-13, 100, 115, 147, 150

National Curriculum
  aims 60-1
  characteristics 62-6
  expressive arts within 59

opera 163
optimism for the future 9, 18-21
out-of-school activities see extra-
  curricular provision
overlapping time pattern 77

part-time specialist staff 149
peripatetic teaching 13, 22, 150
personal experience and arts
  education 13-14, 146
personal growth 66
personal needs, differing 64, 68
polarisation of fine art and design 77
praise 98
preparation period 42-50
'Primary Education in England' (HMI)
  78
primary schools 78, 83, 124
primary teachers 115-16
problem-solving skills 29
progress, assessment of 104, 105
protected time 72
public demands for assessment 91
public support for the arts 164

qualitative vocabulary 45

reactive behaviour 36
recognition of achievement 57, 99
record-keeping and reporting 105-6
'Red Book' see 'Curriculum 11-16'
reflexive behaviour 36, 37
Regional Arts Association (RAA)
  134-5, 138
relevance of curriculum content 65-6,
  68
reports 105, 106
resources
  accommodation 150-1, 158
  allocating 80, 148
  equipment and materials 62-3, 151,
    159
  LEA responsibilities 157-9
  staffing 149-50
rural schools 116, 124

School and College focused In-service
  Teacher Education (SCITE) 120, 121
secondary modern schools 14
secondments 120
self-awareness 31, 33, 35
self-control 33, 37
self-evaluation 103, 106
shared appointments 124
shared assessment policy 153
shortage of teachers 124
single-session visits by artists 142
skills
  acquisition 112, 114
  involved in creative work 29-30,
    102-3
  level of skill mastery 49, 68-9
  teachers' 112, 114-15
social function of the arts 7
source materials 53-4
special educational needs 64, 147
spontaneity of ideas 49
staffing patterns 125, 149
statement of entitlement (LEA arts
  policy) 156
statement of entitlement (school arts
  policy) 8, 147
status of arts within the curriculum
  historic 12-13
  present 9, 20, 96
stimulus
  characteristics 69
  defined parameters 51-2

183

quality of 50–1
relevance 51, 66
subject areas, relationship between 78–9
subject separation 19
susidies 41, 135
syllabus structures 111

targeted funding 17–18
Task Group on Assessment and Testing (TGAT) 93, 94, 105
teacher
  evaluation of performance 106–8
  patterns of employment 126
  role in creative process 42, 54, 55, 58, 81
  shortages 124
teacher performance 106–8
teacher training 20, 24, 113, 114–24, 149–50, 172, 173–4
teacher-pupil relationship 37, 57, 81
team leaders 82–3
team-building 173
technical skills
  realistic level of attainment 48–9
  relevance 48
technical vocabulary 45
Technical and Vocational Education Initiative (TVEI) 17

technological resources 62–3, 110–11, 156
television 34, 37, 38
'The Curriculum from 5–16' 60, 64, 69
time
  allocations 71
  approaches to 72–80
  patterns 73–6, 125–6
timetable, model 81, 84–90
timing of changes 169–70
training
  artists in education 131
  governors 117
  LEA role 122–4
  management 116–17
  teachers 20, 24, 113, 114–24, 149–50, 172, 173–4
training days 121
tri-partite education system 12

understanding of art forms 139–43

visual and audio culture 37–9
visual literacy 38
vocabulary
  acquisition 45–6, 102
  non-verbal 46

writer's residency 142

A companion volume in the
Issues in Education series

School – a place for children?
Henry Pluckrose

In this book Henry Pluckrose examines the approach to education in our schools today and identifies some of the problems and failings. The book is not meant to be seen as a blueprint. It has been written simply to provoke discussion from which the author hopes change can and will grow. It is a book for everyone involved in education – teachers who wish to reassess their professional work, students who wish to look at some of the issues which influence educational progress, thoughtful administrators and politicians who wonder why their labours so often fail to create the schools of their dreams, and parents who have to cope with the consequence of school failure.

Henry Pluckrose, former Headmaster of Prior Western Primary School in London, is now an education consultant in Britain and abroad and is the author of many books for children.

For a complete catalogue of Franklin Watts books for school libraries, please write to:

Franklin Watts Ltd,
96 Leonard Street,
London
EC2A 4RH